MATTHEW ARNOLD

MATTHEW ARNOLD

A STUDY

BY

E. K. CHAMBERS

New York

RUSSELL & RUSSELL

FIRST PUBLISHED IN 1947
REISSUED, 1964, BY RUSSELL & RUSSELL, INC.
L. C. CATALOG CARD NO: 64—15026

PRINTED IN THE UNITED STATES OF AMERICA

CONTENTS

I

ARNOLD'S YOUTH

MATTHEW ARNOLD was born to inherit the purple of Scholarship. The Arnold family were originally of Lowestoft in Suffolk. But Matthew's grandfather William was a Collector of Customs in the Isle of Wight. He seems to have lived firstly at Northwood in West Cowes, and later at Slattwoods, near Whippingham, in East Cowes. He married Martha Delafield, of a family whose origin I have been unable to trace, although some members of it occur in our Matthew's own history. The only one that need concern us is a Frances, the sister of Martha. The poet's father Thomas was the third son of William. Among his sisters were another Frances, who married the Rev. John Buckland, and a Susanna. An elder brother, also a Matthew, went to Corpus Christi College, Oxford, in 1803, became an Army Chaplain, and died in 1820. In 1811 Thomas, at the age of 15, followed him at Corpus. Here an intimate friend was Thomas Trevenen Penrose, son of John Penrose, rector of Fledborough, Notts. At Corpus, too, was John Taylor Coleridge, a nephew of the poet Coleridge, who tells us that already some of the opinions held by Thomas rather startled what was then a markedly Tory college. He was, however, a good scholar, took a First in his final examinations, and in 1815 was elected to a Fellowship at Oriel. In that year also and in 1817 he won the Chancellor's prizes for Latin and English essays. In 1818 he took deacon's orders, after some religious scruples had been removed by conversations with John Keble, then also a Fellow of Oriel. And with these began a friendship which in some sense endured to the end of Arnold's life, although direct intercourse was broken during the greater part of it by a profound divergence of

ecclesiastical opinions. This was notably so during
the Tractarian controversy at Oxford, which began with
Keble's sermon on *National Apostasy* in 1833. Arnold's
theology was then what we should now call Broad
Church. He wanted a comprehensive National Church
which should be in some sense identical with the State,
and should be wide enough to include the Dissenters.
But when Keble visited Rugby as Oxford examiner in
1829 Arnold's children were accustomed to repeat
hymns from Keble's *The Christian Year* at bed-time,
and Arnold was still speaking of 'dear old Keble'. An
intended meeting at Arnold's Westmorland home was
prevented by his sudden death in 1842.

In 1819 Arnold went to live at Laleham on the
Thames near Staines, taking with him his mother, his
aunt Frances, and his sister Susanna. Here he became a
schoolmaster, in partnership with his brother-in-law
John Buckland. Later they seem to have divided their
functions, and Arnold became responsible for the preparation of young men for university life. He had left
Oxford with some regret, especially for its rural sur-
roundings in Bagley Wood and elsewhere. But Laleham
was also in beautiful country, and he long thought it
would be his final home. On 11 August 1820 he married
Mary Penrose, the sister of his old college friend Thomas
Trevenen Penrose. His eldest child was Matthew, born
on 24 December 1822. John Keble was his godfather.
He was followed by four others, Thomas, William Delafield, Edward Penrose, and Walter, and four daughters,
Jane Martha, Mary, Frances (Fanny) Bunsen Trevenen
Whateley, and Susanna. Of these the one who appears
to have been closest to Matthew throughout his life was
Jane Martha, whom he generally, for some unknown
reason, called 'K'. In 1850 she married W. E. Forster,
who became a statesman of considerable repute.

Thomas, the elder, was not destined to remain in-
definitely at Laleham, although his family, especially

Matthew, long preserved their link with it. In 1828 he became Headmaster of Rugby, and set himself to make it a centre both of learning and of Christian life. In 1841 he was elected Regius Professor of Modern History at Oxford, and gave an inaugural lecture there, followed by some others in 1842. He was then thinking of leaving Rugby shortly. He was a good classical scholar, and published an edition of Thucydides and a *History of Rome*, both of repute in their day. Many of his sermons and other miscellaneous writings were printed, some posthumously. These included his *Travelling Journals*. The country around Rugby lacked the charm of Oxford and Laleham, and he gladly escaped from it. During 1825–31, and again in 1837–40, he spent many vacations in France, Italy, Spain, Switzerland, and Germany, sometimes with his wife or in later years with his elder children. This was a taste which we shall find that his son Matthew inherited. And in 1833 he decided to acquire a permanent headquarters. This he found in the Lake country, which offered an additional attraction in the neighbourhood of Wordsworth. After a short stay at Allan Bank in Grasmere, he built himself a house at Fox How near Ambleside, which long remained the home of his widow and a beloved holiday resort of his son. It had been his wish to spend his own declining years there. 'His bones should go to Grasmere churchyard, to lie under the yews which Wordsworth planted, and to have the Rotha with its deep and silent pools passing by.' But he died, quite suddenly, from an attack of *angina pectoris* at Rugby on 12 June 1842.

Of Matthew's earliest days we have little record. Thomas was still young enough to play with his children. He gave them dogs' names and drew up an elaborate set of kennel rules; Matthew was 'Crab'. In 1830 education began under John Buckland. In 1849 he went to Laleham and from there to Pentonhook with his uncle and cousins, 'and all the school following behind, just as I

used to follow along the same river bank eighteen years
ago'. In after life he buried three sons there. It was a
place, he wrote, 'for which I, more than any of us, perhaps, except Jane, shall always have a home feeling'.
From 1833, however, the Lake Country, first from Allan
Bank and afterwards from Fox How, provided an even
more delightful playground. We have an early record
of a tea-party given by Dora Wordsworth to the Arnold
family in the summer of that year on the large island in
Rydal Lake, with Wordsworth himself stretched in the
grass, and Mrs. Wordsworth reading to the elders some
of his manuscript poetry. At Fox How, perhaps a little
later, the children produced and illustrated a *Magazine*,
of which numbers are still existent, both here and in
America. It took frequent occasion to comment on
Matthew's elegance of dress and deportment, and on
his supercilious disdain of the dress and deportment of
his kin.

Matthew's first recorded poem was *Lines Written on the
Sea-Shore at Eaglehurst*. Here, in the Isle of Wight, he was
staying with an aunt during July 1836. He was then
thirteen years of age. In August he was sent to school at
Winchester. From there he walked to Hursley, where
his godfather Keble was rector, and noted his 'flibberti-
gibbet, fanatical, twinkling expression'. In August 1837
he went with his parents and two of the other children
for a short tour in northern France, during which they
visited Rouen, Chartres, Versailles, and Paris. And on
their return Matthew was transferred from Winchester
to Rugby. I am afraid that during his boyhood Matthew
was what may be described in homely parlance as 'a bit
of a lad'. At Winchester he incurred unpopularity by
telling the Headmaster that his work was quite light, and
was pelted by his fellows with 'pontos' in a ritual known
as 'cloister peelings'. Even while in the sixth form at
Rugby, when he displeased Dr. Arnold, and was ordered
to stand behind his chair, he gratified his friends by

making faces over his father's head. This contrasts oddly with his urbanity in later years. Towards the end of his school-days Mary Fletcher of Lancrigg in Grasmere wrote to her mother:

I see that our dear Mrs Arnold's trials are to come from her sons—her standard is so very high and her impression of what their Father's children ought to be so justly elevated, that although to me or you (who have certainly not been accustomed to pattern sons, or brothers or nephews) they seem delightful boys, she is very anxious about them from not tracing the sobriety of mind and manliness of character she has a right to expect from their training. Matt's passion for fishing is as strong as Henry Fletcher's. He is not to be allowed to go to College unless he shows a more decided sense of duty in his school work the next half year. This you sh^d not mention out of our easy chairs.

This letter, the original of which is not now available, is only dated 183–. It may reasonably be ascribed to 1839, in view of a letter by Dr. Arnold on 6 July of that year, in which he writes:

Childishness in boys, even of good abilities, seems to me to be a growing fault, and I do not know to what to ascribe it, except to the great number of exciting books of amusement. . . . These completely satisfy all the intellectual appetite of a boy, which is rarely very voracious, and leave him totally palled, not only for his regular work, which I could well excuse in comparison, but for good literature of all sorts, even for History and for Poetry.

By 26 May 1840, however, Dr. Arnold was planning to stay at Rugby until both Matthew and his brother Tom had gone through the University. Matthew's love of fishing long endured. So did the tendency of his family and friends to shorten his name to 'Matt'.

In 1840 Matthew won a prize at Rugby for a poem on *Alaric at Rome*. In the same year he was elected to an open Classical Scholarship at Balliol. This was supplemented in 1841 by a School Exhibition from Rugby. On

28 November 1840 he had gone up for matriculation. Edward Walford, who was matriculated on the same day, tells us:

I well remember how, when we waited in the Vice-Chancellor's ante-room for admission, Arnold professed to us his great aversion to sundry statements in the Thirty-nine Articles, which at that time we were forced to subscribe, especially that Article which expresses an approval of the Athanasian Creed, and that which denounces and renounces the Pope of Rome.

Apparently he was already developing, and perhaps extending, his father's lines of theological thought. And it was so, too, when he came into residence at Balliol, during the last term of 1841, after a visit with his father to the south of France and the Pyrenees, which he recalled twenty-four years later in the same inn at Fontainebleau. For Walford adds:

In his early days, when we dined at the same scholars' table, I shall never forget how, in opposition to the Tractarianism of the day, he used to say that the strict imposition of creeds had done more to break than to unite churches, and nations, and families, and how even then, in our small and highly privileged circle, he was the apostle of religious toleration in every direction.

Nevertheless, Arnold as an undergraduate was still lighthearted. He had not long been up before he was going out with the Harriers. One Tuckwell records that his leap over the Wadham railings used to be familiar to many who had never read his books. In July 1843 he went for a visit to Devonshire with one J. Manley Hawker, who records that they 'arrived after sundry displays of the most consummate coolness on the part of our friend Matt, who pleasantly induced a belief into the passengers of the coach that I was a poor mad gentleman, and that he was my keeper'. Earlier he had written to John Duke Coleridge, also of Balliol:

Our friend Matt utters as many absurdities as ever, with as grave a face, and I am afraid wastes his time considerably, which I deeply regret, but advice does not go for much with him, and perhaps I am not well qualified to give it.

Walford says that Arnold's cheerfulness, geniality, and universal charity combined to make him as general a favourite at Balliol as he became afterwards in the wider world of society in London. With Benjamin Jowett, then a tutor, he began a friendship which endured to his death. But his own tutor was William Ralph Lingen, with whom he was destined to be concerned in his later career. With his contemporaries I think that there was sometimes an aloofness. J. D. Coleridge once told him that they complained of a lack of interest in them, and he replied:

The accusation, as you say, is not true. I laugh too much, and they make one's laughter mean much too much. However, the result is that when one wishes to be serious one cannot but fear a half suspicion on one's friends' parts that one is laughing, and, so, the difficulty gets worse and worse.

The gift of irony is, no doubt, a dangerous one. Arnold's closest friendships in his undergraduate days seem to have been with Arthur Hugh Clough, whom he had known at Rugby, and who was now at Balliol, until he obtained a fellowship at Oriel in 1842, with Theodore Walrond, also a student at Balliol, and with his own brother Thomas, who came up to University College in 1842. They breakfasted regularly together in Clough's rooms on Sundays. And together they drove their skiffs in the Cherwell and others of the streams around Oxford, or enjoyed delightful wanderings in the Cumnor hills.

In 1843 Arnold won the Newdigate prize with another poem on *Cromwell*. He did not, as has sometimes been stated, win the Hertford Scholarship, but was only a *Proxime Accessit*. In 1844 his final examination in Classics was approaching, and he went to read for it at Fox

How with Clough. On 21 July Clough wrote to a friend:

> For this evening Mat is away; a party of Oxford visitants from Ambleside and Grasmere came over last night to spend the weekly holiday; hospitalities were required, slowdoms to be borne with: so Mat improvised a necessity to visit his Penates, and left the *onus entertainendi* upon me, departing after Morning Services. Mrs Arnold was well and kind, but somewhat anxious about Mat. Mat has done something this week, but this foolish walk to-day will lose him all tomorrow I have no doubt.

Clough is working himself, painfully coerced by the assurance that, should he relax in the least, his yoke-fellow would at once come to a dead stop. Ten days later he adds:

> Matt has gone out fishing, when he ought properly to be working, it being nearly four o'clock. It has, however, come on to rain furiously, so I rejoice to think that he will get a good wetting.

And when they had returned to Oxford in the autumn and the examinations were at hand:

> Matt enters the schools for Paper Work to-morrow. I think he is destined for a Second; this is above his deserts certainly, but I do not think he can drop below it, and one would not be surprised if he rose above it in spite of all his ignorance. However, he has had the wisdom to be perfectly candid to his doctors as to the amount of the disease, and both they and he have been very diligent during the last three weeks.

Seven days later he adds:

> Matt I expect will get a Second; he has just concluded his Paper Work. May he also tread in my steps next Easter!

And a Second it was.

Arnold, however, had a recuperative power. He did redeem his failure of 1844, as Clough hoped he might, by his election to a Fellowship at Oriel on 28 March 1845. This gave much pleasure to Wordsworth, 'who had taken

Matt under his special protection as a 2nd classman'. In the interval he had been taking a class at Rugby under his father. But he had now to leave this for a probationary year of residence in college. This probably began in April 1845 and ended in March 1846. In September 1845 he paid a visit to the Isle of Man and Ireland with his mother and his sister Jane. About this time he developed an interest in the theatre, which he never wholly lost. It began with an enthusiasm for the French actress Élisa Félix Rachel. In his article on *The French Play in London* (1879, *Irish Essays*), he wrote:

I remember how in my youth, after a first sight of the divine Rachel at the Edinburgh Theatre, in the part of Hermione, I followed her to Paris, and for two months never missed one of her representations.

There may be some lapse of memory here. Apparently Arnold's diaries of this time, now at Yale, give no evidence of a visit to Edinburgh. But in July 1846 Rachel was playing in London, and here Arnold may easily have seen her. In August his probationary year at Oriel was over, and he was able to spend a considerable period abroad. But his first object was to see the French writer George Sand, in whose books he had also taken an early interest. He gives an account of his visit to her in an article of 1877 (*Mixed Essays*). By rail and diligence he made his way to Boussac in the French province of Berry, and from here he wrote to George Sand at her Château of Nohant, conveying the homage of a foreigner and offering a visit. It was accepted. He found a large party, including the musician Chopin.

She conversed of the country through which I had been wandering. Of the Berry peasants and their mode of life, of Switzerland, whither I was going.

Probably they also talked, in connexion with Switzerland, of Étienne Pivert de Senancour, the author of *Obermann*, who was recently dead, and whom George

Sand had edited. When Arnold reached Switzerland he probably found himself in localities much haunted by Senancour. So at least we may infer from the opening words of his *Obermann Once More*, which may well have been written in 1866,

> Glion?—Ah, twenty years, it cuts
> All meaning from a name!

Later Arnold became, at least for a time, disenchanted with George Sand. In 1859 he was unwilling to take a long journey 'to see such a fat old muse'. But in 1876 he records of that one and only meeting that she said of him to Ernest Renan, 'Je lui faisais l'effet d'un Milton jeune et voyageant,' and adds, 'She was the greatest spirit in our European world from the time that Goethe departed.'

After his return from Switzerland Arnold went to Paris, as his diaries show, on 29 December 1846. Here he saw Rachel the same night in *Polyeucte*, and had seen her at least ten times before he left for England on 11 February 1847.

On his return to Oriel Clough wrote to John Campbell Shairp,

> Matt is full of Parisianism; theatres in general, and Rachel in special: he enters the room with a chanson of Béranger's on his lips—for the sake of French words almost conscious of tune: his carriage shows him in fancy parading the Rue de Rivoli; and his hair is guiltless of English scissors: he breakfasts at 12, and never dines in Hall, and in the week or 8 days rather (for 2 Sundays must be included) he has been to Chapel *once*.

He was a member of the Decade, a debating society, mainly composed of Oriel and Balliol men. His residence at Oxford was not prolonged. About April 1847 he became private secretary to Lord Lansdowne, then President of the Council in Lord John Russell's ministry. His brother Thomas wrote to Clough: 'I quite agree with you in disliking the notion of this appointment for

Matt.' We do not know why. He had, of course, now
to live in London. Perhaps they saw tendencies in him
which they thought that contact with the great world
might unduly stimulate. Mrs. Arnold, however, wrote
from London in 1850:

> Matt has been with us almost every day since we came up,
> and it is pleasant indeed to see his dear face, and to find him
> always so affectionate, and so unspoiled by his being so much
> sought after in a kind of society entirely different from anything
> we can enter into.

He continued, of course, to be a Fellow of Oriel until his
marriage in 1851. We get a final picture of him from
Friedrich Max Müller, who first visited Oxford in 1847.
It can hardly rest on much first-hand knowledge of his
early days.

> He was beautiful as a young man, strong and manly, full of
> dreams and schemes. His Olympian manners began even at
> Oxford; there was no harm in them. The sound of his voice and
> the wave of his arm were Jove-like.

II

THE PUBLIC SERVANT

ARNOLD's employer from about April 1847 to about
April 1851 was Henry Petty-Fitzmaurice, Marquis
of Lansdowne, an old statesman, who was President of
the Council during Lord John Russell's Liberal ministries
from 1846 to 1852. The appointment, of course, necessi-
tated residence in London, where probably Arnold
lodged at 101 Mount St. His letters of this period are
merely dated from London or sometimes from Lansdowne House. To his employer he often refers as 'my
man'. Lansdowne had also a country house at Bowood
Park in Wiltshire, where Arnold expected to be in
December 1849. The duties of a secretary were not so
arduous as to leave no time for holidays, and in the Sep-
tembers of 1848 and 1849 Arnold was able to visit Switzerland. His experiences there must be matter for another
chapter, and if he was at Bowood in December 1849, he
was also at Fox How shortly before Christmas. Edward
Quillinan tells Henry Crabb Robinson of his arrival
there on 18 December. On 2 January he was dining with
Quillinan. He was there again in May 1850. Crabb
Robinson describes him as 'a very gentlemanly young
man, with a slight tinge of the fop that does no harm
when blended with talents, good nature and high spirits'.
Doubtless his salary was not large. Quillinan hesitated to
ask him to join a committee for establishing a memorial
to Wordsworth, then lately dead, 'as perhaps the naming
him might involve a subscription, however moderate'.

In 1850 Arnold fell in love with Frances Lucy, the
daughter of Sir William Wightman, a Judge of the Court
of Queen's Bench. Clough wrote to his brother Thomas
on 23 July:

Matt comes to Switzerland in a month; after your sister's

wedding. He is deep in a flirtation with Miss Wightman, daughter of the Judge. It is thought it will come to something, for he has actually been to Church to meet her.

Thomas himself records a 'counterblast' in his relations with her, which drove him out of England and towards the Alps. It was the family belief that he secretly followed the Wightmans in a trip to the Continent. There may be some confirmation of this in his poem *Calais Sands*, written in August 1850, a copy of which he apparently sent to the lady. She is coming to Calais:

> I must not spring to grasp thy hand,
> To woo thy smile, to seek thine eye;
> But I may stand far off, and gaze,
> And watch thee pass unconscious by.

And again:

> To-morrow hurry through the fields
> Of Flanders to the storied Rhine!
> To-night those soft-fringed eyes shall close
> Beneath one roof, my queen! with mine.

The roof was probably that of an hotel at Calais, where Arnold and his wife stayed in later years. Presumably the 'counterblast' was the refusal by Judge Wightman to allow an engagement with his daughter, on the ground that Arnold had not a sufficient and secure permanent income. As a means of obtaining this Arnold's thoughts turned to an Inspectorship in the Department of Education, of which Lord Lansdowne, as President of the Council, was the nominal head. William Ralph Lingen, who had been his tutor at Balliol, and, he says, 'a genius of good counsel to me ever since', and was now Secretary to the Committee of Council on Education, gave him advice and on 14 April 1851 Lansdowne appointed him as an Inspector. Wightman now gave his consent to the marriage, which took place on 10 June 1851 and was followed by a tour in Italy, which Arnold recalled when he visited the same district in 1865.

Drs. Tinker and Lowry print a letter to Wyndham Slade, in which Arnold says that for the fifth time the deities had interposed. He had been asked specially to meet the young lady, but when he mounted the stairs he learnt that at the last moment her mother had been given tickets for the opera and had sent a note of excuse. He was suffering from great dejection and lassitude in consequence. He goes on to plan a journey abroad with Slade. Spain would be too hot before October, and by the middle of that month 'they' wanted him, but the Pyrenees or Savoy and the Italian lakes might do. I take it that 'they' must mean the Education Office. He concludes:

How strange about *die unerreichbare schöne*! To have met her, to have found something *abstossend*, and to have been freed from all disquietude on her account, *voilà comment je comprends* a matter of this kind. But all the oppositiveness & wilfulness in the human breast is *agaçée* by a succession of these perverse disappointments. Farewell, *denke mein*.

I find this rather cryptic. Probably it was written in 1851 between April, when Arnold got his appointment, and June, when the marriage took place. No doubt the idea of a foreign trip with Slade was dropped when Wightman gave his consent to the marriage. In later letters Arnold's wife generally becomes 'Flu', perhaps to avoid confusion with his sister, also a Fanny.

Arnold remained an Inspector of Schools to 1886. It is important to remember that practically the whole of his work as a writer and lecturer was done against the background of strenuous service as an officer of the State. And for that purpose a brief account of the early development of the Education Office as an organ of national administration is desirable. Attempts in the earlier part of the nineteenth century to pass a Bill for a contribution from State funds towards the education of the children of the masses had been defeated by the opposition of the House of Lords. After the Reform Bill of 1832 the need for such provision came to be more widely felt, and in 1833 the difficulty was surmounted by proceeding not through a Bill, but through a Vote on Supply in the House of Commons, with which the Lords could not constitutionally interfere. The amount voted was £20,000 in aid of private subscriptions for the erection of School Houses. It was payable to a National Society for Church Schools and a British and Foreign Schools Society for Nonconformist Schools. In 1835 an additional £10,000 was voted for Training Colleges for Teachers. In 1839 a Committee of Privy Council on Education was established with the Lord President of the Council as its official head and a Secretary of its own. The post was held to 1849 by James Kay, later Sir James Kay-Shuttleworth, and after him by W. R. Lingen to 1869 and Francis Sandford to 1884. By an Order in Council of 1839 the Committee laid it down that no further grants should be made either to Training Colleges or to other schools, unless they accepted inspection, in order to secure conformity to regulation and discipline, and for this purpose a body of Inspectors was appointed later in the same year. They were not to interfere directly with religious instruction, which was left to the ecclesiastical authorities, or with discipline and management, but to collect facts and information and make their reports to the Committee. In 1846 their number was increased. At the same time pupil teachers were introduced to help the adult staff of the schools, while continuing their own education until they entered Training Colleges, and it became part of the duty of the Inspectors to examine them. In 1856 a comprehensive Education Department was established to comprehend the functions both of the Committee of the Privy Council and of an establishment for the encouragement of Science and Art, formerly under the Board of Trade. At the same time a Vice-President of the Committee of Council was appointed to represent the Department in Parliament.

In 1860 the various Orders in Council and Minutes affecting education were reduced into the form of a Code. Then, too, a Royal Commission under the Duke of Newcastle recommended a searching examination of every pupil in the indispensable elements of knowledge, on which the prospects and position of the teachers were largely to depend. And now trouble began. The views of the Commission were accepted by Robert Lowe, then Vice-President of the Committee, who attempted to incorporate them in a revised Code, which was further revised in 1862. Grants to schools were now to be based, as to two-thirds on the individual examination of pupils over 8 years of age in reading, writing, and arithmetic, which came to be known as 'the three R.s', and as to one-third only on the total number of children found by the Inspector to be in regular attendance at the school concerned. This system of 'payment by results' in fact lasted for over thirty years, and only died an unregretted death in the nineties. At the time of its introduction it was much disliked by Kay-Shuttleworth and by the Inspectors, who sent a protest to Lord Granville, then President of the Council. To Arnold's share in the controversy which it evoked we shall have to return. In 1864 Lowe had to resign after a vote of censure in the House of Commons for alleged mutilation of Inspectors' Reports, from which a Select Committee of the House later exonerated him. In 1870 a new Act, introduced by W. E. Forster, then Vice-President of the Committee, established local School Boards, with the duty of securing an adequate provision of Elementary Schools and the power of financing them out of the rates.

Arnold entered upon his new responsibilities in a mood of optimism. To his wife he wrote from Manchester on 15 October 1851:

I think I shall get interested in the schools after a little time; their effects on the children are so immense, and their future efforts in civilising the next generation of the lower classes, who,

as things are going, will have most of the political power of the
country in their hands, may be so important. It is really a fine
sight in Manchester to see the anxiety felt about them, and the
time and money the heads of their cotton-manufacturing population are willing to give to them. In arithmetic, geography and
history the excellence of the schools I have seen is quite wonderful, and almost all the children have an equal amount of information; it is not confined, as in schools of the richer classes, to
the one or two cleverest boys. We shall certainly have a good
deal of moving about; but we both like that well enough, and
we can always look forward to retiring to Italy on £200 a year.
I intend seriously to see what I can do in such a case in the
literary way that might increase our income. But for the next
three or four years I think we shall both like it well enough.

For several years his range of inspection was a wide one.
He seems to have had a headquarters at Derby, where he
lodged with one Sansom at Babington Hall. But we find
him at work, during 1851 to 1854, not only in the mid-
lands of Warwickshire, Oxfordshire, Worcestershire, and
Bedfordshire, but also in the eastern counties of Lincoln,
Norfolk, Suffolk, Huntingdon, and Cambridge, and as
far north as Manchester, west as Shropshire, and south as
Sussex. In London he visited the early Training College
at Battersea. In 1856 he was hoping for a change which
would limit him to London, Middlesex, and Kent. But it
is not clear that any came before 1871, when he writes:

They are proposing for me a *perfect* district: *Westminster*, and
a small rural district round Harrow. And I have made no
application, said not a single word.

Apparently his responsibilities were thenceforward to
include Church Schools, for in another letter he says:

There are great regrets in that part of my district which I am
leaving. My success has been due entirely to a naturally, I
hope, humane manner, and then to the sense of my entire fairness. I shall be rather curious to see what will be my experience
in dealing with clerical managers; they will certainly be less
interesting, because so much more what one has been familiar

with all one's life. But I imagine also they will be more inclined
to expect to have the law a little strained in their favour, and
less content with plain absolute fairness than the Nonconformist
managers.

Arnold once said, 'No one shall say that I am a punctual
Inspector.' But it is clear that he was an efficient one.
And even more interesting is his reference here to his
'humane manner'. There is an echo of this in 1867, when
he wrote to his mother:

> What I like best is such a letter as I saw the other day in the
> Council Office, not meant for me to see, from a teacher defend-
> ing his school against a severe report of mine; he finished by
> saying that he had not a word against the inspector, whom he
> would rather have than any other he had ever come in contact
> with, 'as he was always gentle and patient with the children'.
> The great thing is *humanity* after all.

It is clear that during several years at least Arnold's life
as an Inspector was an arduous one. When in London
he had for some time no settled abode. We find his wife
with him at Derby, probably in October 1853, and
certainly in November 1854. But mostly she appears to
have continued to live with her parents in London at
38 Eaton Place, and here, or at Teddington, where
Justice Wightman also had a place, her husband could
sometimes join her. In February 1855 he was hoping to
be settled in London, and for a time took a house at
11 Belgrave Street, although the pair continued to 'dine
in our old fashion every night in Eaton Place'. This did
not last long. In December 1856 Eaton Place seems again
to have been his headquarters. But he occasionally
escaped from it to work or write letters at 'my old rooms',
presumably during his private secretary days, at 101
Mount St., now occupied by his friend Wyndham Slade,
a barrister. During the summers of 1856 and 1857 he was
staying, with his wife, for short periods at Brighton,
Folkestone, Dover, and Hampton-on-Thames. In February 1858 he took a house at 2 Chester Square. 'It is a

very small one,' he wrote, 'but it will be something to unpack one's portmanteau for the first time since I married, now nearly seven years ago.' In 1866 he had let this, and was living in a house at West Humble, Dorking, but in the spring of 1868 moved from 'the dear little house' to Byron House at Harrow. It had great advantages. The offices were bad, but there was ample space for a spare bedroom, dressing-room, and bachelor's room, and 'a good library for me, which is a great blessing'. And there was a garden. In 1871 the Duke of Genoa, who was a son of King Vittorio Emanuele II of Italy, was living with him here, and on his departure. Arnold was given in reward the Order of Commander of the Crown of Italy. He remained at Harrow until 1873, when he moved to Pains Hill Cottage at Cobham in Surrey, which was his home for the rest of his life.

The routine of inspection he seems, for a considerable time, to have found exhausting, both from the amount of travelling it involved, and from the exacting details of paper work for which he was responsible. Early in December 1851 he records a hard day, with 'thirty pupil-teachers to examine in an inconvenient room, with nothing to eat except a biscuit, which a charitable lady gave me'. Later in the same month he was sore put to it with new schools opening, and 'tooth ache and other incommodities'. A year later he says:

This is one of the most uncomfortable weeks I ever spent. Battersea is so far off, the roads so execrable, and the rain so incessant.

From Cambridge in 1853 he writes:

I have had a long tiring day, and it certainly will be a relief when I get these Eastern Counties over. The worst of it is that invitations to go and see schools are *rained* upon me; and managers who have held out till now against the Government plan ask me on my father's account to come and inspect them, and to refuse is hard.

And in 1854 from Oxford:

I am just back from Witney; as cold and uncomfortable a life I have had since I left you as one could desire. My bedroom here is fust and frowsiness itself, and last night I could not get to sleep.

A month or two later, from London:

I am not very well lately, have had one or two things to bother me, and more and more have the feeling that I do not do my inspecting work really well and satisfactorily; but I have also lately had a stronger wish than usual not to vacillate and be helpless, but to do my duty, whatever that may be; and out of that wish one may always hope to make something.

So too in 1859:

I am overwhelmed with grammar papers to be looked over, and not choosing as I grow older, and my time shortens, to give up my own work entirely for any routine business, I have a hard time of it just at present. When I have finished these papers I have a General Report and a Training School Report to get out of hand, the inspection of schools going on alongside of this all the while, so at the beginning of next month, when my office work is again reduced to inspecting, I shall feel myself quite a free man.

A little later he rejoices in the offer of a job abroad:

You know that I have no special interest in the subject of public education, but a mission like this appeals even to the general interest which every educated man cannot help feeling in such a subject. I shall for five months get free from the routine work, of which I sometimes get very sick, and be dealing with its history and principles.

He went, and no doubt relished the experience. But on his return he describes four continuous days of examination at the Westminster Training School, with eighty candidates to look after, and gas burning most of the day, either to give light or to help warm the room. In 1862 he describes an even more terrible programme. He inspected, again at Westminster, from ten to a quarter past two, then had lunch, and after it did another school.

Then I got home, and went out immediately to get my daily snuff of air, foggy stuff as it is. I am just returned, and after this is written I must report on a heavy school, which will take me till dressing time. We dine in Eaton Place, where they have one or two people. We shall be back here about a quarter past ten, then I shall report on a light school, write two or three letters, read about a hundred lines of the *Odyssey* to keep myself from putrefaction, and go to bed about twelve.

In 1863 the work he most dislikes in the world is looking over and marking examination papers. His eyes trouble him. But he has a moment of qualified optimism.

All this is a busy life, but I am very well and enjoy it. Inspecting is a *little* too much as the business half of one's life in contradistinction to the inward and spiritual half of it, or I should be quite satisfied.

I omit some later groans.

More than once he had hopes of getting some easier official post, which led to nothing. In 1866 he applied for a vacant Charity Commissionership, but a lawyer was required. In 1867 he hoped for the Librarianship of the House of Commons, with the encouragement of both Gladstone and Disraeli, only to find that 'a horrid domestic intrigue' among the officials of the House stood in the way. In 1869 another Commissionership under the Endowed Schools Act seemed possible, but on this occasion Gladstone himself was the obstacle. In 1882 he felt that Gladstone would never promote the author of *Literature and Dogma*, and that it was time to think about retiring. He was much surprised in 1883, when Gladstone offered him a Civil list pension of £250 a year, 'as a public recognition of service to the poetry and literature of England', but he accepted it after some hesitation. He was on good personal terms with his official chiefs, although Lingen he came to think a bore, and he did not like his wife much. More congenial to him, however, was Sir Francis Sandford, who came to the office in 1848 and succeeded Lingen as head of it in 1869. He was 'a far better fellow than Lingen and has real geniality'. He recognized, nevertheless, that Lingen was 'one of the best and most faithful of public servants'.

There were some amenities in the life of the early Inspectors of Education which did not pass to those of later years. Arnold's responsibilities did not prevent him from acting as Marshal to his father-in-law Sir William Wightman when he went on official tours as a Judge. And the Inspectors were allowed a considerable freedom in the public expression of their personal views on educational topics. There was a notable example of this during the controversy on Lowe's *Revised Code* in 1862. Arnold fully shared the dislike of Kay-Shuttleworth and of the Inspectorate in general for this, although he recognized the good intentions of Lowe, whom he thought 'an acute and brilliant man, to whom pretentiousness with unsoundness was very distasteful and contemptible'. In September 1861 he began an article of protest, which was not finished until March 1862, when it appeared in *Fraser's Magazine* as *The Twice Revised Code*. Later, in 1887, he wrote an account of the whole controversy. He knew in 1862 that he was taking some risks, but thought his comment on Lowe would be found vivacious, and that he had 'done something to ward off the heaviest blow dealt at civilisation and social improvement in my time'. He found, however, that Lord Granville, then President of the Council, shared his views, and that his protest was welcomed, not only by Kay-Shuttleworth and, as perhaps might have been expected, by his brother-in-law W. E. Forster, but also by others, who felt that the State has interest in the primary school as a *civilizing agent*, even prior to its interest in it as an *instructing agent*. He recognized that the chiefs of his office would be incensed against him.

I don't think, however, they can eject me, though they can, and perhaps will, make my place uncomfortable. If thrown on the world I daresay we should be on our legs again before very long. Any way, I think I owed as much as this to a cause in which I have now a deep interest, and always shall have, even if I cease to serve it officially.

But Arnold was by now too valuable a servant of the State to be thrown overboard. By June 1862 the revised code was dead, and Lingen and his wife were dining with him. 'They were both very amiable, and not the least allusion was made to the Code.' In fact Arnold's efficiency was by this time too great to be dispensed with. I have noted his mission abroad in 1859. The results of this he was allowed to publish in book form during 1861, as *The Popular Education of France, with Notices of that of Holland and Switzerland*. A Preface to it was reprinted in his *Mixed Essays* in 1879. Two others were to follow. In 1865 he was sent to France, Italy, and Germany on behalf of a Schools Inquiry Commission. The result was his *Schools and Universities on the Continent* of 1868. Here he was dealing, not with Elementary Schools, for which alone his Office was responsible, but with education of a more advanced type. On this he had already touched in his *A French Eton* of 1864, of which he said: 'I have written, to my own mind, nothing better.' The need for a sounder education of the middle classes had now become a prominent feature in his speculations on English civilization in general. In 1866 he wrote:

The truth is, I see nothing except a Secretaryship for Middle Class Education which would really suit me, under my circumstances, better than the post I hold.

His third mission took place just before his retirement, which he had contemplated in 1882, but in fact deferred to 1886. It was done at the request of his Office and took him once more to France and Germany, for an inquiry into their systems of Free Schools. A collection of some of Arnold's *Reports* was made by Lord Sandford in 1889, and another, with a preface by F. S. Marvin, was issued by the Board of Education in 1908.

III

ARNOLD AND CLOUGH

ARTHUR HUGH CLOUGH was born at Liverpool on
1 January 1819. His father, James Butler Clough, of
an old Welsh family, migrated to Charleston, U.S.A.,
about 1823. Arthur was, however, sent to school in
England, first at Chester in 1828, and then at Rugby,
under Dr. Arnold, in 1829. In 1837 he went to Balliol,
and after a failure to take a First Class in his final examination became a Fellow of Oriel in 1842, and Tutor in
1843. In 1848 he resigned both posts, went to Paris
during the hectic days of the French Revolution, then to
Rome by 1849, where he witnessed the siege of the city by
the French, and in the autumn became Principal of the
un-sectarian residence for students at University Hall in
London. He had early relations with Ralph Waldo
Emerson and Thomas Carlyle. In 1850 he visited
Venice. He found himself uneasy in his post and in 1850
tried unsuccessfully for one at Sydney in Australia, and
also apparently in 1851 for one in the Education Office.
In 1852 he resigned his Principalship and went to Cambridge, Massachusetts. Here he became a journalist and
began a revision of Dryden's translation of Plutarch's
Lives, which was not published until 1859. In 1853 he
returned to England to take up an Examinership in the
Education Office which had now become available for
him. In 1854 he married Blanche Smith, a cousin of
Florence Nightingale, in whose social work he took much
interest. He had now seven years of comparative quiet,
and continued his Plutarch. Three children were born
to him. In 1856 he acted as Secretary to a Commission
on Continental Military Schools. In 1859 his health broke
down. In search of recovery he went to Malvern in 1860,
to the Isle of Wight in February 1861, to Greece and

Constantinople in April, returned to England in June, travelled again, this time with Alfred Tennyson, in Auvergne and the Pyrenees in July, joined his wife at Paris in September, and from there went to Switzerland and the Italian lakes, meaning to reach Florence and to winter in Rome. But at Florence he was attacked, first by malarial fever and then by paralysis, and there he died on 13 November. His grave is in the Protestant cemetery, outside the city gates.

Clough, like Arnold, was a poet. His *The Bothie of Toper-na-Fuosich*, later called *Bothie of Tober-na-Vuolich*, was published in 1848. In 1849 he collaborated with Thomas Burbidge in an *Ambarvalia*. In the same year he wrote his *Amours de Voyage* at Rome, but this did not appear until 1858, when it was printed in the *Atlantic Monthly*. His *Dipsychus*, begun at Venice in 1850, his *Mari Magno* and his *Songs in Absence* of 1852 and 1853, together with many miscellaneous short pieces, were collected by his friend F. T. Palgrave in *Poems, with a Memoir* (1862) and again by his widow in *Poems and Prose Remains, with some Letters and a Memoir* (1869).

I have already noted, in the chapter on *Arnold's Youth*, the close relations between Arnold and Clough in their Oxford days. The friendship between them endured to the end. Its story is best told in H. F. Lowry's *The Letters of Matthew Arnold to Arthur Hugh Clough* (1932), although some additions can be made from other sources. They were in many ways of different tempers. Clough's life was destined to be an unhappy one. There was a morbid strain in him. As an undergraduate he sought for truth, 'like a straw drawn up the draught of a chimney'. He was full of self-questioning and mastered by doubts on religion, which he could neither frankly accept nor completely throw off. He never, like Arnold, arrived at a working philosophy of things. And so he remained an attractive but rather ineffective personality to the end. In his early days he was much attracted by John Henry

Newman and Hurrell Froude. But he never became a Tractarian. A friend wrote to him in 1843:

> You seem to be in the midst of the Oxford heresies without having suffered much beyond a good puzzling.

Later he was influenced by relations with Thomas Carlyle and the American Ralph Waldo Emerson. He was a frequent speaker at the Decade. Frederick Temple in 1862 recalled a speech on the future politics of the world, the connexion of the world and of the Church. He said the grandeur of the thought and the splendour of the language quite carried him away. He had great influence over his younger contemporaries, but disliked using it.

> Once Dr. Temple had expressed some opinion, when Clough said, 'Why, you thought differently six months ago.' Dr. Temple said, 'Yes, but you knocked that out of me.' He remembered the kind of shrinking when Arthur heard that.

He became troubled at the obligation upon University men of subscribing to the Thirty-nine Articles of the Church of England, and though he signed them, a recurrence of the scruple led him to resign his Fellowship and Tutorship at Oriel in 1848.

> It irk'd him to be here, he could not rest.
>   He loved each simple joy the country yields,
>   He loved his mates; but yet he could not keep
>   For that a shadow lower'd on the fields,
>   Here with the shepherds and the silly sheep.
>   Some life of men unblest
>   He knew, which made him droop, and fill'd his head.
>   He went; his piping took a troubled sound
>   Of storms that rage outside our happy ground;
>   He could not wait their passing, he is dead!

And so, 'Thyrsis of his own will went away.'

Of the letters in Lowry's collection all but one are from Arnold himself. Only two can be as early as 1845. Three or four are of 1847. Arnold's epistolary style is at first rather stilted and affected. He, too, I think, had not yet quite found himself. He was wearing a shell. He was himself conscious of it. About 1851 he writes of his wife:

You'll like my Lucy; she has all my sweetness and none of my airs.

Even in 1853 he is still not quite natural.

I am past thirty, and three parts iced over.

The letters of 1845 show both Arnold and Clough already interested in the novels of George Sand. Those of 1847 criticize poems by Clough, some of which were later to appear in the *Ambarvalia*. Arnold has read them with some reluctance, but on the whole thinks that they will stand grandly, with Burbidge's 'barbaric ruins' smirking around them. Later he apologizes for 'a beastly vile note'. He had not done justice to the great precision and force Clough had attained in inward ways. But perhaps Clough should be on his guard against his own individuality.

The longest series of letters, eighteen in all, comes in 1848. At the beginning of it Arnold is still writing on poetry. He has little opinion of Burbidge, who 'lives quite beside the true poetical life, under a little gourd'. He has a growing sense of the deficiency of the *beautiful*, as distinct from the rhetorical, devotional, or metaphysical, in Clough's verse. But aesthetics now give way to politics. It was the year of the French Revolution, which at its opening excited Clough more than Arnold. In March he wrote to a friend:

If it were not for all these blessed revolutions, I should sink into hopeless lethargy.

Arnold took it more calmly. In a letter to his sister Jane he says:

I was myself tempted to attempt some political writing the other day, but in the watches of the night I seemed to feel that in that direction I had some enthusiasm of the head perhaps, but no profound stirring. So I desisted, and have only poured forth a little to Clough, we two agreeing like two lambs in a world of wolves.

Another letter he addressed to Citizen Clough, Oriel Lyceum, Oxford. But the Revolution stirred him to the beginning of those studies on the organization of society which were later to exercise him so frequently.

Certainly the present spectacle in France is a fine one: mostly so indeed to the historical swift-kindling man, who is not haunted by the pale thought, that, after all man's shiftings of posture, *restat vivere*.

He thought the eternal relations between labour and capital, of which *The Times* twaddled, had small existence for a whole society that has resolved no longer to live by bread alone. Later he notes the '*wide and deep-spread intelligence* that makes the French seem to themselves in the van of Europe'. In March the French Provisional Government was established under Lamartine and others. Arnold wrote to his mother and to Clough on an article by Carlyle.

How deeply restful it comes upon one, amidst the hot dizzy trash one reads about these changes everywhere. The source of repose in Carlyle's article is that he alone puts aside the din and whirl and brutality which envelop a movement of the masses, to fix his thoughts on its ideal indivisible character.

To Clough he added:

Carlyle says, I am told,—'The human race has now arrived at the last stage of Jack assification.'

He reads George Sand's *Lettres au Peuple*.

I do not like it so well as at first. For my soul I cannot *understand* this violent praise of the people. I praise a fagot where-of the several twigs are nought: but a *people*?

In April the example of France gave encouragement to the Young Ireland party, which contemplated rebellion against English rule. Arnold thought that the mass of people in England would not see much bloodshed in Ireland without asking themselves what they were shedding it to uphold. An abortive Chartist demonstration in London followed. Arnold now met Emerson, who was staying with Clough and went with him to Paris in May. Arnold remained in England, reading Goethe and noting his 'thorough sincerity, writing about nothing that he had not experienced'. In June or July he commented on the Italian rising against Austrian rule. 'I am divided', he wrote, 'between a desire to see those cursed poltroons the Lombards well kicked—and to have so ugly a race as the Germans removed from Italy.' With the French he was now disenchanted. 'The New Gospel is adjourned for this bout.'

He was now much concerned at Clough's resignation of his Oriel Fellowship, and was busy in thinking of jobs for him. Some tutorships in private houses were open, and a post in the Education Office was also a possibility. Arnold, however, went to Switzerland in the autumn, and Clough to the English Lakes. On his return he wrote his *The Bothie*. Arnold is critical of it.

I have been at Oxford the last two days and hearing Sellar and the rest of that clique, who know neither life nor themselves, rave about your poem, gave me a strong, almost bitter, feeling with respect to them, the age, the poem, even you. Yes, I said to myself, something tells me I can, if need be, at last dispense with them all, even with him: better that, than be sucked for an hour even into the Time Stream in which they and he plunge and bellow. I became calm in spirit, but uncompromising, almost stern. More English than European, I said finally, more American than English: and took up Obermann, and refuged myself with him in his forest against your Zeit Geist.

Still, he is glad to learn that the poem is selling well.

The Bothie and the *Ambarvalia* and Arnold's own *Strayed Reveller* volume, both of which followed it early in 1849, seem to have turned his mind again from politics to poetry. 'The millennium, as Matt says, won't come this bout', wrote Clough. Arnold's comments on his own verses will best find their place in another chapter. He is anxious to know what Clough thinks of his *Resignation*. 'Tell me freely, if you do not like it.' Here comes Lowry's one letter from Clough, written at Rome on 23 June, during the bombardment of the city by the French.

Why the devil I should write to you he only knows who implanted the spirit of disinterested attention in the heart of the spaniel.

These are damned times, replies Arnold. Carlyle is a moral desperado.

In a letter of 1849 to Thomas Arnold, Clough had said:

Do we not work best by digging deepest? by avoiding polemics, and searching to display the real thing? If only one could do the latter! Emerson is an example, and also Carlyle, and, in his kind, M. A.

In 1850 and 1851 he is back in London. The friends often breakfast together, but there are naturally few letters. But in 1852 there is something of a rift between them. Arnold was now married. In March Clough writes to his fiancée Blanche Smith:

Tonight I go to meet Mr and Mrs Arnold again; they leave town tomorrow. Considering that he is my most intimate friend (or has been) it is not a great deal to have seen of him during ten days that he has been here and hereabout, to have spent an hour with him at a theatre last evening: well perhaps a couple of hours more this evening at a party? I like the wife very well,—more, the more I see of her; Nevertheless?

In April Arnold writes:

I called at Doubting Castle the very day you escaped from it. I took it very ill you did not come and dine that day in Eaton Place—the . . . ye have always with you, but me ye have not always. However all will be forgiven you if you obey me now. From Rugby you will come and see me at Derby, at my expense. Now this must absolutely be, therefore resign yourself.

Doubting Castle is, of course, University Hall. Clough told Blanche Smith he supposed he must go, but did not. Arnold said he was sincerely disappointed not to see him, but supposed it was inevitable. In August 1852 the friends took a holiday together in Wales. By the end of October Clough had resigned Doubting Hall and was starting for America. Arnold wrote:

I have got your note: Shairp, I hope, will come to me for a day, and then he can bring the money.

As to that article, I am anxious to say that so long as I am prosperous, nothing would please me more than for you to make use of me, at any time, as if I were your brother.

Lowry, rather oddly, says that the 'article' was Clough's prospective review of Arnold's *Poems* of 1852, which appeared in the *North American Review* for July 1853. But surely it was money. Arnold was helping to finance his friend's voyage. In December he acknowledges a letter from Clough, and bids him not to write scraps across the Atlantic. He wants a nice long letter or he will dry up as a correspondent. In February 1853 he did get a letter from Clough, but it was disappointing. He is not sure that he can answer it as he wishes. A rather long analysis is necessary. He had not thought that Clough had been permanently hurt by anything he had done or left un-done while they were in London together. He was then absorbed in his speculations and plans and agitations respecting Fanny Lucy, and was as egoistic and anti-social as possible. He had told Clough this and thought that he realized it. He never, while they were both in London, had any feeling towards Clough but one of attachment and affection. He remembered an occasion on which Clough had been vexed at not finding him when he expected it, but thought that he had explained how it was. At one time, indeed, shortly after Clough's publication of *The Bothie*, he had felt a strong disposition to intellectual seclusion and the barring out all influences

that he felt troubled without advancing him, but the
charm and salutary effect of Clough's company and
mode of being had overcome this.

In short, my dear Clough, I cannot say more than that I really
have clung to you in spirit more than to any other man—and
have never been seriously estranged from you at any time—for
the estrangement I have just spoken of was merely a contemplated one and it never took place.

He contemplated writing more on the next day, but
decided not to go on with it. But he did add a little.

The period of my development coincides with that of my
friendship with you so exactly that I am for ever linked with
you by intellectual bonds—the strongest of all: more than you
are with me: for your development was really over before you
knew me, and you had, properly speaking, come to your *assiette*
for life.

He would go and call on Blanche Smith. In March 1853
he had an answer from Clough, which is not preserved.
'We will not discuss what is past', he wrote. But apparently Clough was not satisfied. In May Arnold says:

I do not know that the tone of your letters exactly facilitates
correspondence—however, let it be as you will. I do not think
we did each other harm at Oxford. I look back to that time
with pleasure.

He thinks Clough will come all right, when he is once
married. After Clough's return from America in July to
take up a post in the Education Office, Arnold writes:

I said nothing while we were together about the subject of
your letters—or many of them—because I thought there was no
need so to do. We will leave the past to itself—for the present
I can sincerely say that I never felt more strongly than now—
or so strongly—how close I am to you—and, in my own feeling,
to you alone.

The remaining letters of 1853, when they are not on
the affairs of the Education Office, are again mostly on

poetry. There are few in later years. Arnold, in 1859, whenever he composes anything, still cares for Clough's opinion beyond that of anyone else. His last letter is in July 1861, four months before Clough's death at Florence. He tells his mother of the loss he feels and the deep impression Clough made on him. He does not feel able to publish anything upon him yet, but hopes some day to relieve himself of what he thinks about him. To a friend he wrote:

I cannot say his death took me altogether by surprise—I had long had a foreboding something was deeply wrong with him. But the impression he left was one of those which deepen with time and such as I never expect again to experience.

In the course of 1862, winding up his Oxford Lectures on Homer, Arnold carried out the intention he expressed to his mother.

How, then, can I help being reminded what a student we have just lost in Mr Clough? He, too, was busy with Homer; but it is not on that account that I now speak of him. Nor do I speak of him in order to call attention to his qualities and powers in general, admirable as these were. I mention him because, in so eminent a degree, he possessed these two invaluable literary qualities,—a true sense for his object of study, and a single-hearted care for it. He had both; but he had the second even more eminently than the first. He greatly developed the first through means of the second. In the study of art, poetry, or philosophy, he had the most undivided and disinterested love for his object in itself, the greatest aversion to mixing up with it anything accidental or personal. His interest was in literature itself; and it was this which gave so rare a stamp to his character, which kept him so free from all taint of littleness. In the saturnalia of ignoble personal passions, of which the struggle for literary success, in old and crowded communities, offers so sad a spectacle, he never mingled. He had not yet traduced his friends, nor flattered his enemies, nor disparaged what he admired, nor praised what he despised. Those who knew him well had the conviction that, even with time, these literary arts would never be his. His poem, of which I before spoke, has some admirable Homeric qualities; out-of-doors frankness, life, naturalness, buoyant rapidity. Some of the expressions in that poem,—'*Dangerous Corrievreckan . . . where roads are unknown to Loch Nevish*,'—come back now to my ear with the true Homeric ring. But that in him of which I think oftenest is the Homeric simplicity of his literary life.

This is a long quotation, but it shows Arnold at his best. The poem quoted is *The Bothie*. To Mrs. Clough he wrote, thanking her for some lines by her husband, which he would take to Oxford, where he could think of him as he wished, 'among the Cumner hills where we have so often rambled'. *Thyrsis*, of course, did not appear until 1866. But it had been for some time in contemplation. In 1863 Arnold wrote to his mother,

The weather was fine but with a detestable cold wind, so that a new poem about the Cumner hillside, and Clough in con-nexion with it, which I meant to have begun at Oxford this week, I could not begin. I have been accumulating stores for it, however.

In 1866 he told her that the diction of the poem was modelled on that of Theocritus, whom he had been read-ing during the two years in which it had been forming itself, and was meant to be so artless as to be almost heed-less. The images were all from actual observation. The cuckoo was heard in a garden at Woodford. He thought it was probably too quiet a poem for the general taste but would stand wear. A little later he added,

It had long been in my head to connect Clough with that Cumner country, and when I began I was carried irresistibly into this form; you say, truly, however, that there is much in Clough (the whole *prophet* side, in fact) which one cannot deal with in this way, and one has the feeling, if one reads the poem as a memorial poem, that not enough is said about Clough in it; I feel this so much that I do not send the poem to Mrs Clough. Still Clough *had* this idyllic side too; to deal with this suited my desire to deal again with that Cumner country: anyway, only so could I treat the matter this time. *Valeat quantum.*

He is, of course, linking the poem in his mind with the *Scholar-Gipsy*. In 1868 he refused Mrs. Clough's request that he would write a set memoir of her husband, feeling so disinclined to the task that he was sure he would not do it well.

IV

THE POET

MATTHEW ARNOLD was a poet from boyhood. I have already noted his *Lines Written on the Sea-Shore at Eaglehurst* in 1836. It is not necessary to be elaborate about this, or about the academic exercises of *Alaric at Rome* and *Cromwell*, which won him prizes at Rugby in 1840 and at Oxford in 1843. In the library of the University of Yale at New Haven, Connecticut, U.S.A., is preserved a large collection of his poetic manuscripts and autograph letters, including what is more specifically known as the *Yale Manuscript*, on the title-page of which is now written,

Unpublished poems, notes on lectures, and other matter, in the handwriting of Matthew Arnold, contained in a note book used by the poet at Balliol College, Oxford, 1843.

It has been pointed out by C. B. Tinker and H. F. Lowry, in their valuable *The Poetry of Matthew Arnold, A Commentary* (1940) that this title is rather misleading. The *Yale Manuscript* is really a collection of first drafts of poems, unfinished fragments of others, and notes for possible future composition. Some of these are of later date than 1843. Tinker and Lowry think that this date may only refer to the particular fragment found on the same page, which they call from its opening words *Rude Orator*. Arnold made use of some of this material for his published volumes of 1849 and 1852. They suggest that another fragment which they call *The Pillars of the Universe* may have been intended for a Song of Callicles in *Empedocles On Etna* (1852). A third they call *To Meta: The Cloister*, and think that its suggestion is taken up in *Stanzas from the Grande Chartreuse* (1855). The *Yale Manuscript* also has a list of possible subjects for poems, headed 'Comp. 1849', with some notes of the themes to be dealt with under each title. These begin

Chew Lucretius
Compose

Among the titles are 'Empedocles', 'Eugenia', 'To Antonia', 'To Meta', 'Thun', 'Shelley-Spezzia', 'Narcissus', 'Sonnets'. The editors attempt to trace in some of these a relation to extant poems, chiefly from Arnold's volumes of 1849 and 1852. But if any of these were written in 1849 it must have been quite early in the year, as the volume was published by 26 February. Yet I do not see that 'Comp.—Compose' can mean 'already composed'. Tinker and Lowry say that other lists of work to be composed are found in Arnold's note-books. These he seems to have been in the habit of compiling year by year to the end of his life, and noting in them books he intended to read and passages from those he had read and which had struck him. The passages are in many tongues, Greek, Latin, Italian, German, French, as well as English. I do not find any notes for the composition of poems in the examples from 1852 to 1888 published in 1903 by his daughter Eleanor. She says the practice of keeping such books lasted thirty-seven years. From earlier examples Tinker and Lowry have been able to date, at least approximately, the composition of some eight poems, largely sonnets, in 1844–8. Most of these appeared in the volume of 1849. A letter from Arnold's brother Thomas suggests that *The New Sirens*, also in that volume, was written by 1847.

The most interesting of Arnold's early schemes is that for a poem on Lucretius. The 'Chew Lucretius' of 1849 was preceded by notes in reading-lists of 1845 and 1846, and followed by others in 1855, 1856, and 1858. It was in 1858 that he discussed Lucretius during his inaugural lecture as Professor of Poetry at Oxford. Tinker and Lowry print some fragments intended to form part of the poem. Another was used as preface to the reprint of

Thyrsis in 1867. It is described as from 'Lucretius, an unpublished Tragedy'. This remained unpublished, and indeed unwritten, to the end. On 29 December 1855 Arnold wrote to Wyndham Slade,

I am full of a tragedy of the time of the end of the Roman Republic—one of the most colossal times of the world, I think. It won't see the light, however, before 1857.

Slade notes,

The idea of writing a poem of the Roman Republic period was not carried out. I do not know that it was begun. He spoke to me about it.

On 17 March 1866 Arnold wrote to his mother,

I am rather troubled to find that Tennyson is at work on a subject, the story of the Latin poet Lucretius, which I have been occupied with for some twenty years. I was going to make a tragedy of it, and the worst of it is that every one, except the few friends who have known that I had it in hand, will think I borrowed the subject from him. So far from this, I suspect the subject was put into his head by Palgrave, who knew I was busy with it. I shall probably go on, however, but it is annoying, the more so as I cannot possibly go on at present so as to be ready this year, but must wait till next.

Twenty years later, on 13 January 1886, he wrote to Goldwin Smith,

One or two things in verse, which all my life I have wished to do, I am now probably too old to do well. One of them is a Roman play, with Clodius, Milo, Lucretius, Cicero, Caesar in it.

We should have been glad to compare Arnold's handling of Lucretius with that of Tennyson.

Arnold's first volume of poems was published, as already noted, by 26 February 1849. It took its title, *The Strayed Reveller and Other Poems*, from its longest piece, of 297 lines; *The New Sirens* has 278, *Resignation* 276, *The Sick King in Bokhara* 232. Three others, *Mycerinus*, *The Forsaken Merman*, and the *Fragment of an Antigone* run to

more than 100. The rest, making up in all twenty-
seven poems, are shorter. *The Strayed Reveller, Resignation,
Mycerinus,* and *The Forsaken Merman* have much poetic
charm, in whole or in parts. *The New Sirens,* as Arnold
admitted to Clough, is 'a mumble'. Another letter to
Clough suggests that at one time he meant to complete
the *Antigone.* 'My Antigone supports me and in some
degree subjugates destiny', he said. But he never did.
There are eleven sonnets. Some are of early date. Four
are notable. The first, which opened the volume, is
there only headed *Sonnet.* It begins,

> One lesson, Nature, let me learn of thee,
> One lesson that in every wind is blown,
> One lesson of two duties serv'd in one,
> Though the loud world proclaim their enmity,
> Of Toil unsever'd from Tranquillity.

In 1853 it was treated as the motto for Arnold's poems
as a whole. In 1869 it was renamed *Quiet Work.* In later
editions it again opened the volumes. Tinker and Lowry
take this as evidence that Arnold regarded it as of primary importance with respect to his poetry and to his
philosophy of life. The sonnet *To A Friend,* probably
Clough, to whom Arnold sent some lines from it in 1848,
praises three writers as propping his mind in bad days.
They are Homer, Epictetus, and finally Sophocles,

> whose even-balanc'd soul
> Business could not make dull, nor Passion wild:
> Who saw life steadily and saw it whole:
> The mellow glory of the Attic stage;
> Singer of sweet Colonus, and its child.

A third, which echoes this, is *To the Duke of Wellington* :

> Laborious, persevering, serious, firm;
> For this, thy track, across the fretful foam
> Of vehement actions without scope or term,
>   Call'd History, keeps a splendour, due to wit,
>   Which saw *one* clue to life, and follow'd it.

A fourth is to Shakespeare:

> Self-school'd, self-scann'd, self-honour'd, self-secure.

Mycerinus is half in six-line stanzas and half in blank verse. *Resignation* is in four-foot iambic couplets. But in contrast to these standard forms Arnold also made use, in *The Strayed Reveller* itself and in many other poems throughout the volume, of a very irregular metrification, with stanzas of varying length, occasional unrhymed lines, and stresses which are often not iambic, but trochaic, dactylic, or anapaestic. He was experimenting in lyrical form, largely, I suspect, under the influence of the Greek tragic choruses.

I have noted Arnold's praise in his sonnets of those who can see life steadily and see it whole. He has already in 1849 an image for the course of human life, of which he was to make considerable use later. It is like the course of a river. *In Utrumque Paratus* is an address to Man, as one born in a 'sacred world', which had its origin in 'the silent mind of One all pure'.

> O waking on a world which thus-wise springs!
> Whether it needs thee count
> Betwixt thy waking and the birth of things
> Ages or hours: O waking on Life's stream!
> By lonely pureness to the all-pure Fount
> (Only by this thou canst) the colour'd dream
> Of Life remount.

In *Resignation* the Poet describes to his companion Fausta the wisdom of those who have conquered Fate and now can draw homewards to the general life.

> The world thinks them foolish, but they are not so in His eye,
>
> > To whom each moment in its race,
> > Crowd as we will its neutral space,
> > Is but a quiet watershed
> > Whence, equally, the Seas of Life and Death are fed.

It is perhaps a little cryptic.

Something more must be said of *Resignation*. It is the last poem in the volume, and seems to have been much in Arnold's mind during 1849. He quotes a line of it to Clough, perhaps in February, and says in March,

I must hear some day how you feel about *Resignation*. Tell me freely if you do not like it.

It describes two walks, taken no doubt from Rydal or Grasmere, and passing over Dunmail Raise to the Nag's Head Inn at Wythburn, and then by the Armboth and Watendlath Fells to a town, which is evidently Keswick, and in the case of the first walk on to the sea, presumably at Maryport. The first walk is by a motley band under a leader, the second, in a July, only by Arnold, with a companion Fausta, to whom the poem is dedicated. There is much beauty in the description of the life which the walkers see around them. Less notable are the comments on the attitudes to that life ascribed to Fausta, to a Poet, and to a band of Gipsies whom they pass by. Arnold's philosophy of life is as yet only tentative. The walks were no doubt real ones, but there is some confusion as to their dates. On 7 August 1849 Arnold's brother Thomas wrote to his mother,

Does Fausta mean K., and is the walk ten years ago that which we took over Wythburn Fells to Keswick with Captain Hamilton? Or was no particular walk intended?

I have no doubt that Fausta was K., the usual term by which Arnold addresses his sister Jane. She is Fausta again in the dedication of one other poem in 1849, but never before or after. Jane Arnold married W. E. Forster in 1850, but he had visited Mrs. Eliza Fletcher at Lancrigg, near Grasmere, about December 1848, and Jane Arnold may then have become engaged to him. The Captain Hamilton referred to by Thomas Arnold is traceable as a friend of Wordsworth's in the Lakes, as early as 1832. He was a Thomas Hamilton, who had been in the army during his youth. In 1833 he

was living at Rothay Cottage in Rydal. Later he married
Lady Farquhar, and moved to Elleray on Lake Winder-
mere. Some confusion as to the date of *Resignation* has
been caused by a memorial stone which now stands near
the Nag's Head Inn at Wythburn. It gives the dates of
Arnold's birth and death, and puts those of the two
walks in 1833 and 1843 respectively. The date of death
might, of course, have been a later addition. That Arnold
could have written anything so good as *Resignation* in
1843 I cannot believe. I do not remember seeing any
such memorial stone when I haunted the country round
Grasmere during my youth. And none is recorded in the
edition of Baddeley's *English Lake District*, published in
1909. Through the kindness of Mrs. Rawnsley, I have
been able to see a letter of Arnold's sister Frances,
written from Fox How on 14 January 1916. From it I
take the following extracts:

> I have no personal memories of Allan Bank. I was only six
> weeks old when I went there in December 1833. . . . My parents
> went to Allan Bank first in July 1833, that was the time when
> the walk was taken recorded by my brother's poem of Resigna-
> tion, he was then eleven and a half years old. . . . My father
> saw Southey at Keswick that summer and had 'a very friendly
> interview with him'.

I suspect that it was on some such evidence as this that
the Wythburn memorial stone was dated. Tinker and
Lowry accept its dating. But they add that 'Arnold's
note of 1869 speaks of the "sedentary landlord of thirty
years ago"'. I have a copy of the 1869 volume and what
it says is 'twenty years' ago. It is 'thirty years' in 1881,
and I daresay in 1877, although I have not the edition of
that year. Probably the 'twenty' then became 'thirty',
owing to the further lapse of time. The exact wording
of 1869 is as follows:

> Those who have been long familiar with the English Lake-
> Country will have no difficulty in recalling, from the description
> in the text, the roadside inn at Wythburn on the descent from

Dunmail Raise towards Keswick, its sedentary landlord of twenty years ago, and the passage over the Wythburn Fells to Watendlath.

Twenty years before 1869 takes us to 1849, not 1843. It is true that the sedentary landlord is related in *Resignation* to the first walk rather than the second, but he may well have been still there in 1849. I put the first walk in 1838, when we cannot trace Arnold's movements, and the second in July 1848, when the family seems to have been at Fox How before Matthew went to Switzerland. It must be added that there was a visit to Keswick in 1833, which may have confused Frances Arnold's recollection of her childhood. It is recorded in Mrs. Eliza Fletcher's *Autobiography*. She has just been discussing her friendship with the Arnolds, and then inserts a letter of 26 July 1833, in which she had written:

> On Wednesday afternoon we set forth to Keswick. Miss Southey followed us to the side of the lake with an invitation to drink tea with them. We all went.

Probably the 'we all' includes at least the adult Arnolds. This confirms the statement of Frances Arnold, in the letter of 1916 already quoted. But the walkers can hardly have gone on to the sea after tea-time.

The *Strayed Reveller* volume was much in Arnold's mind during 1849. He wrote to his sister Jane, complaining that he had not heard what she thought of it. It was selling well, and had evoked interest in a good many quarters, although everyone liked something different, except that everyone liked the *Merman*. There were complaints at Oxford that the subjects treated did not interest readers there. But as he felt rather as a reformer in poetical matters, he was glad of that opposition.

> More and more I feel bent against the modern English habit (too much encouraged by Wordsworth) of using poetry as a channel for thinking aloud, instead of making anything.

Later he adds, in substance:

Fret not yourself to make my poems square in all their parts.
They are fragments. I am fragments, while you are a whole.
A person who has any inward completeness can at best only
like parts of them. They stagger weakly and are at their wits
end. I shall do better some day, I hope.

And finally, apparently in May:

I have many poetical schemes, but am fermenting too much
about poetry in general to do anything satisfactory. My last
volume I have got absolutely to dislike.

To Clough he wrote from Thun in September that he was
getting to feel more independent and unaffectible as to
all intellectual and poetic performance, the impatience
at being *faussé* in which drove him some time since so
strongly into himself, and more snuffing after a moral
atmosphere to respire in than ever before in his life.

Arnold's second volume did not appear until 1852,
probably about October, when he wrote to Wyndham
Slade that he had published some poems which, out of
friendship, he forbore to send him. The title *Empedocles
on Etna and Other Poems* was again taken from the longest
poem, with which the volume opened. It is divided into
acts and scenes, and has 1,121 lines. *Tristram and Iseult*,
in three parts, has 774. Into it was inserted in 1869 a
part of *Lines written by a Death-Bed*, the rest of which had
already become *Youth and Calm* in 1867. The only other
poems of 1852 longer than 100 lines are *The Youth of
Nature*, *The Youth of Man*, and *Obermann*. This last can
perhaps be best discussed in connexion with Arnold's
philosophy. All these longer poems have passages of
considerable beauty, although perhaps they do not represent any great advance from those of 1849. There is
still a good deal of Arnold's irregular metrification. But
there is also a considerable group of short poems, mostly
in simple four-foot iambic quatrains, with alternating
rhymes. There are only two sonnets. *Obermann*, with its

reference to Wordsworth, had been written as early as November 1849. The noble *Memorial Verses* on his death had appeared in *Fraser's Magazine* for June 1850. 'I have dirged Wordsworth *in the grand style*', wrote Arnold to Clough. There is much more of him in *The Youth of Nature*, a beautiful thing throughout. A list of poems to be done, which is dated by Tinker and Lowry as of 1851, can hardly be later than 1849, since it includes the 'Obermann Stanzas', as well as *Empedocles* and *Tristram and Iseult*, and some other things which did not appear until 1853, although they must have been long in Arnold's mind. One contemplated subject, *Hylas*, he seems never to have used.

In several poems of the 1852 volume we get again the metaphor of human life as a water to be traversed, which has already been noted in 1849. In *Human Life* we are 'charter'd by some unknown Powers', and 'stem across the sea of life by night'. In *Self-Dependence* the poet is,

> Weary of myself and sick of asking
> What I am, and what I ought to be,
> At the vessel's prow I stand, which bears me
> Forwards, forwards, o'er the starlit sea.

In *A Summer Night* most men live and die in a brazen prison. Only a few,

> Escape their prison and depart
> On the wide Ocean of Life anew.

Even the freed prisoner may hold some false way and become a driving wreck:

> Is there no life but these alone?
> Madman or slave, must man be one?

In *The Buried Life* Fate gave man a chance of obeying his genuine self, even in his own despite,

> Bade through the deep recesses of our breast
> The unregarded River of our Life

> Pursue with indiscernible flow its way;
> And that we should not see
> The buried stream, and seem to be
> Eddying about in blind uncertainty,
> Though driving on with it eternally.

It is perhaps only 'when a beloved hand is laid in ours' that a man becomes aware of his life's flow.

> And then he thinks he knows
> The Hills where his life rose,
> And the Sea where it goes.

In *The Youth of Man* a couple stand by night, looking down on a still valley and city spires,

> And there in the dusk by the walls,
> With the grey mist marking its course
> Through the silent flowery land,
>   On, to the plains, to the sea,
> Floats the Imperial Stream.

For a moment the mists of delusion fall from their eyes, and they feel how Nature was fair. The metaphor is not always quite consistently used, but a sense of the flux of things is always recurring in Arnold's mind.

In the end he became as dissatisfied with his second volume as he had been with his first. He found weight in what he wrote but little or no charm.

> I feel now where my poems (this set) are all wrong, which I did not a year ago: but I doubt whether I shall ever have heat and radiance enough to pierce the clouds that are massed round me.

Incidentally he recorded that not more than fifty copies of the volume had been sold.

It is in connexion with the volume of 1852 that we can best consider what I once called the 'enigmatic figure' of Marguerite. Her story seems to me simpler now, although rather complicated by Arnold's varying arrangements of the poems relating to her at different dates, and occasional alterations of their texts. Arnold, according to his daughter Lady Sandhurst, always insisted in after-life that Marguerite was imaginary. What else can a pater-familias say when his children question him as to the object of his early love poems? Marguerite was a very real person. We get a chronological background in two letters to Clough. On 29 September 1848 Arnold wrote from the Baths of Leuk that he had been over the Simplon to Domo d'Ossola, and on the morrow should repass the Gemmi and get to Thun. Here he should 'linger one day at the Hotel Bellevue for the sake of the blue eyes of one of its inmates', before starting on a leisurely journey back to England. On 23 September 1849 he says, from Thun itself, 'I wrote to you from this place last year.' And he adds,

I am here in a curious and not altogether comfortable state: however tomorrow I carry my aching head to the mountains and to my cousin the Blümlis Alp.

Then he quotes from his poem *Parting* ten lines, which end,

I come, O ye mountains!
Ye torrents, I come!

And finally he comments,

Yes, I come, but in three or four days I shall be back here, and then I must try how soon I can ferociously turn towards England.

Thun is in that part of Switzerland which lies south of Basle and the Rhine. To it the river Aar runs down from Berne, and then turns to the east, passing through two lakes, those of Thun itself and that of Brienz, with the village of Interlaken between them. The old town of Thun is dominated by a Schloss, below which a steep street leads to the lake. In it is the Hôtel Bellevue et du Parc. At the foot of the street a covered bridge leads to an island. From the Schloss you can see the Blümlis Alp

in the distance. Farther south is the Rhône, flowing west
to the Lake of Geneva, with Geneva itself at its west end,
and Vevey, Glion, and Chillon at the east. Between the
area of the Aar and that of the Rhône are the Bernese
Alps, in which are the Blümlis Alp and the Gemmi Pass.
On the Rhône is Leuk, and to the south of the river are
the Valais, the Simplon Pass, and Domo d'Ossola, from
which you can reach Piedmont and Italy. With all this
country Arnold was familiar.

It is to Thun·that the episode of Marguerite belongs.
The first notice of her in verse is in the *To my Friends who
Ridiculed a Tender Leave-Taking* of 1849. One of its nine
stanzas runs as follows,

> Marguerite says: 'As last year went,
> So the coming year'll be spent:
> Some day next year, I shall be
> Entering heedless, kiss'd by thee.'
> Ah! I hope—yet once away,
> What may chain us, who can say?
>   Ere the parting kiss be dry,
>   Quick, thy tablets, Memory.

This refrain is repeated at the end of each stanza. It is
notable that in 1857 its first line was altered to

> Ere the parting hour go by.

The poem tells of many a broken promise, then new
made, to break again. Marguerite is not named in *The
Voice*, but there can be little doubt that the voice was hers.
A contemporary suggestion by Wyndham Slade that it
was that of Arnold's father may be safely rejected. Again
a textual alteration helps us.

> In vain, all, all in vain,
> They beat upon mine ear again,
> Those melancholy tones so sweet and still;
> Those lute-like tones which in long distant years
>   Did steal into mine ears:

Blew such a thrilling summons to my will
  Yet could not shake it:
Drain'd all the life my full heart had to spill;
  Yet could not break it.

When *The Voice* was reprinted in 1877, Arnold substituted 'in the bygone year' for 'in long distant years', and that is, no doubt, what he originally wrote.

The list in the *Yale Manuscript* of poems for composition in 1849 includes *Thun,* with an addition on 'vividness of sight and memory compared'. Tinker and Lowry note the echo here of the lines in *To my Friends,*

If the clear impression dies,
Ah! the dim remembrance prize!

In the volume of 1852 there are four poems which name Marguerite in the text or a title. They are *The Lake* (later called *Meeting*), *Parting, Absence, To Marguerite In Returning a Volume of The Letters of Ortis.* To these must be added *A Farewell,* which does not name her, but about which there can be no doubt. Her voice recurs in *Parting.*

But on the stairs what voice is this I hear,
Buoyant as morning, and as morning clear?
Say, has some wet bird-haunted English lawn
Lent it the music of its trees at dawn?
Or was it from some sun-fleck'd mountain-brook
That the sweet voice its upland clearness took?

In 1853 Arnold grouped these poems, with the omission of *A Farewell,* under the heading of *Switzerland,* called the Ortis poem simply *To Marguerite,* and added *A Dream,* in which he sailed, with a Martin, down an Alpine stream, seeing Marguerite, with an Olivia, on the balcony of a cottage as he passed, and was then carried from them by the River of Life to the Sea. We know no more of Martin and Olivia. Possibly they were the *Friends* of the 1849 poem. In 1854 he restored *A Farewell.* In 1857 he added another poem *To Marguerite,* and called that on the Ortis letters *Isolation.* In the first collected edition of

1869 the *To Marguerite* of 1857 is *Isolation, To Marguerite,* and the Ortis poem is now *To Marguerite Continued. To my Friends* becomes *A Memory-Picture. A Dream* is dropped.

Professor H. W. Garrod, in his *Poetry and the Criticism of Life* (1931) calls the volume of 1852 'Marguerite's book, the book of forsaken or separated lovers'. I do not dissent from this description, although I think that he goes rather far in finding traces of the episode in some of its miscellaneous contents. I do not quite agree in his statement that the collection 'has a somewhat surprising unity, the unity, I feel, of a single and intense experience'. It has other topics, such as that of Wordsworth, with which Marguerite is not concerned. I do not find a very clear parallel to her story in *Tristram and Iseult.* A Margaret is in *The Forsaken Merman,* but that is of 1849.

It is in the 1869 order of the *Switzerland* grouping that the course of Marguerite's relations with Arnold, except for the omission of *A Dream,* is most continuously to be traced.

In *To my Friends* there has been kissing and she expects more next year. Arnold may have expressed a doubt, and she murmurs 'Art thou still unkind?'

> Many a broken promise then
> Was new made—to break again.

But in *Meeting* he does return, with a scruple as to the wisdom of it.

> Again I spring to make my choice;
> Again in tones of ire
> I hear a God's tremendous voice—
> 'Be counsell'd and retire!'

In *Parting* he is 'bound for the mountains', no doubt the Blümlis Alp. The voice and look of Marguerite almost stay him, but he realizes the impossibility of linking his life to hers.

> A sea rolls between us—
> Our different past!

And she has already had other lovers. The fullest account of the breach is in *A Farewell*. He rides, presumably after his return from the Blümlis Alp, beside the lake, past the poplar avenue and the roofed bridge, and up the steep street to where he sees her taper's beam. They are clasped in each other's arms. But soon he discovers a trouble in her altered air.

> Thy hand lay languidly in mine—
> Thy cheek was grave, thy speech grew rare.

He realizes that the episode is over.

> I blame thee not :—this heart, I know,
> To be long lov'd was never fram'd.

Some day perhaps he and she may come near each other again,

> And greet across infinity.

As he anticipated to Clough, he ferociously returned to England. In *Absence* a 'fair stranger's eyes of grey' recall Marguerite's to him.

> I shudder : for the passing day
> Had borne me far from thee.

The two poems, each of which in its turn became *Isolation*, were presumably written after his return to England. I do not think that either of them was sent to Marguerite, although one was suggested by the discovery that he had brought away her Ortis book, and must return it to her. Both are philosophical reflections on the theme that 'we mortal millions live alone'. *The Terrace at Berne* was written after a visit to that town in 1859. He thought of Thun, not far away, but did not go there. Would Marguerite greet him?

> Or hast thou long since wander'd back,
> Daughter of France! to France, thy home;
> And flitted down the flowery track
> Where feet like thine too lightly come?

Doth riotous laughter now replace
Thy smile, and rouge, with stony glare,
Thy cheek's soft hue, and fluttering lace
The kerchief that enwound thy hair?

I do not think that this stanza was worthy of Matthew
Arnold.

Or is it over?—art thou dead?—
Dead?—and no warning shiver ran
Across my heart, to say thy thread
Of life was cut, and closed thy span!

Could from earth's ways that figure slight
Be lost, and I not feel 'twas so?
Of that fresh voice the gay delight
Fail from earth's air, and I not know?

Or shall I find thee still, but changed,
But not the Marguerite of thy prime?
With all thy being re-arranged,
Pass'd through the crucible of time?

With spirit vanished, beauty waned,
And hardly yet a glance, a tone,
A gesture—anything—retain'd
Of all that was my Marguerite's own?

I will not know!—for wherefore try
To things by mortal course that live
A shadowy durability
For which they were not meant, to give?

It was a brief experience, but a very real one, while it
lasted. Two other poems, not in the *Switzerland* series,
contain reminiscences of the parting with Marguerite
and of the trouble which it caused Arnold. One, from
the 1852 volume itself, is in *A Summer Night*. He is in a
deserted moon-blanched street.

And to my mind the thought
Is on a sudden brought
Of a past night, and a far different scene.
Headlands stood out into the moon-lit deep
As clearly as at noon;
The spring-tide's brimming flow
Heav'd dazzlingly between;
Houses with long white sweep
Girdled the listening bay:
Behind, through the soft air,
The blue haze-cradled mountains spread away.
  That night was far more fair;
But the same restless pacings to and fro,
And the same vainly-throbbing heart was there,
And the same bright calm moon.

The other is in *A Southern Night*, published much later, in 1861.

Ah, such a night, so soft, so lone,
  So moonlit, saw me once of yore
Wander unquiet, and my own
  Vext heart deplore!

Of Marguerite herself we get a fairly consistent picture. Besides her voice, she had a slight figure of pliant grace, a pale sweet-rounded cheek, lovely lips with an arched smile, a chin the archest mockery ever ambushed in, soft hair bound in a lilac kerchief, and above all, several times referred to, sweet eyes, so blue, so kind. But to her eyes I must return later. She was not illiterate, since she could read the *Lettere di Jacopo Ortis*, either in the French translation (1847) of Ugo Foscolo's work, or in an English one of 1814. Probably she was a visitor at the Hôtel Bellevue, rather than a serving-maid.

One other point I must note here. In a lecture of 1931 I was inclined to put to the account of Marguerite not only the *Switzerland* group of poems, but also another which in 1855 Arnold brought together as *Faded Leaves*. I now think I was wrong, and that these are related to

Arnold's courtship of Miss Wightman about 1850, although perhaps the interval was rather short for them to fade in. Here were five poems. Four of these, *The River*, *Too Late*, *On the Rhine*, and *Longing*, had appeared in the volume of 1852. *Separation* was added in 1855 itself. I am not sure that this, with its reference to 'the sure consolations of Time', was not originally written on Marguerite. It ends,

> Then, when we meet, and thy look strays towards me,
>> Scanning my face and the changes wrought there,—
> *Who*, let me say, is *this Stranger regards me*,
>> *With the grey eyes, and the lovely brown hair?*

And though, as I have already said, Marguerite's eyes were blue, Miss Wightman's eyes in *On the Rhine* come rather near to that.

> Those eyes of deep soft lucent hue—
>> Eyes too expressive to be blue,
>> Too lovely to be grey.

And, on the other hand, in the Marguerite poem of *Absence* we get,

> In this fair stranger's eyes of grey
> Thine eyes, my love, I see.

Are lovers always so uncertain as to the colours of their mistresses' eyes? Some others of the 1852 poems might belong either to Marguerite or to Miss Wightman, for example, *Excuse*, *Indifference*, and *The Buried Life*, with its reference to 'a beloved hand laid in ours'.

Arnold's discontent with his two earlier volumes did not prevent him from publishing a third in 1853. It contained much salvage both from 1849 and from 1852. I have noted already the grouping here of the Marguerite poems, with the addition of *A Dream*, in *Switzerland*. From 1849 came *Mycerinus*, *The Strayed Reveller*, *The Forsaken Merman*, and the *Nature* and *Shakespeare* sonnets, and from 1852 *Tristram and Iseult* and *The Future*, but only one

fragment of *Empedocles*, here called *Cadmus and Harmonia*.
Several minor things from both sources were allowed to
survive. It is rather surprising to me that *Resignation* was
omitted. There were also several new poems, of which
the most important are *Sohrab and Rustum*, *The Church of
Brou*, with a Marguerite in it, *The Scholar Gipsy*, and
Requiescat. Here we get some of Arnold's best work.
Oddly enough, *The Scholar Gipsy* did not quite satisfy
him. In November 1853 he wrote to Clough:

> I am glad you like the Gipsy Scholar—but what does it *do* for
> you? Homer *animates*—Shakespeare *animates*—in its poor way
> I think Sohrab and Rustum *animates*—the Gipsy Scholar at best
> awakens a pleasing melancholy. But this is not what we want.
>
> > The complaining millions of men
> > Darken in labour and pain—
>
> What they want is something to *animate* and *ennoble* them—not
> merely to add zest to their melancholy or grace to their dreams
> —I believe a poetry of this kind is the basis of my nature—and
> of my poetics.

'My poems, however,' he adds, 'viewed *absolutely*, are
certainlyʻ little or nothing.' One may perhaps doubt
whether the complaining millions of men are very likely
to be much animated by poetry. Later he thought better
of *The Scholar Gipsy*. To Wyndham Slade he wrote in
1854 that he was exploring the Cumnor country and had
got into one of the little coombs that his father had been
so fond of, and which he had in his mind in the *Gipsy
Scholar*, and felt the peculiar *sentiment* of the country and
neighbourhood as deeply as ever. And so, too, to his
brother Thomas in 1855,

> What you will like best, I think, will be the Scholar Gipsy. I am
> sure that old Cumner and Oxford country will stir a chord in you.

And again in 1857,

> You alone of my brothers are associated with that life at
> Oxford, the *freest* and most delightful part, perhaps, of my life,

when with you and Clough and Walrond I shook off all the
bonds and formalities of the place, and enjoyed the spring of life
and that unforgotten Oxfordshire and Berkshire country. Do
you remember a poem of mine called *The Scholar Gipsy*? It was
meant to fix the remembrance of those delightful wanderings of
ours in the Cumner hills, before they were quite effaced,—and
as such Clough and Walrond accepted it, and it has had much
success at Oxford, as was perhaps likely from its *couleur locale*.
On Tuesday afternoon I smuggled myself away and got up into
one of our old coqmbs among the Cumner hills, and into a field
waving deep with cowslips and grasses, and gathered such a
bunch as you and I used to gather in the cowslip field on Lutter-
worth road long years ago.

Sohrab and Rustum, which runs to 892 lines, is certainly a
fine span of blank verse, and Arnold was justified in his
satisfaction with it, although personally I prefer him in
his more lyrical moods. Probably he had it in mind as
early as 1851, since 'The Death of Sohrab' occurs in the
list, already noted, of subjects for poems, some of which
had been used in 1852. There, too, is 'La châtelaine
architecte', which is probably *The Church of Brou*. It is
doubtless *Sohrab and Rustum* of which he wrote to his sister
Jane, in April 1853, as a thing which gave him more
pleasure than anything he had done yet. A month later
he said much the same both to his mother and to Clough,
and called the story 'a very noble and excellent one'.
He thought that his treatment of it had, if not the *rapidity*,
at least the *fluidity* of Homer.

In a Preface to the volume of 1853 he gave his reasons
for not reprinting *Empedocles* in full. He had not omitted
it because he thought that he had failed in the delineation
which he intended to effect. But Empedocles belonged
to a late period of Greek philosophy, when the influence
of the Sophists had begun to prevail. The calm, the
cheerfulness, the disinterested objectivity of the early
Greek genius had disappeared, modern problems had
presented themselves. 'We hear already the doubts, we

witness the discouragement, of Hamlet and of Faust.'
He admits, with Aristotle, that any accurate imitation or
representation gives pleasure. It is the basis of our love
of Poetry. But if the representation is a poetical one
more is demanded. It must not only interest, but also
inspirit and rejoice the reader, must convey a charm and
infuse delight. Even a tragic representation may do this.
What then are the situations from the representation of
which, though accurate, no poetical enjoyment can be
derived? They are those in which suffering finds no vent
in action, in which there is everything to be endured,
nothing to be done. The representation of these in poetry
is painful, not tragic. Such a situation he now thought
that of *Empedocles* to be, and therefore he omitted the
poem.

The volume of 1853 was reprinted in 1854, with the
omission of *The Youth of Man* and *A Modern Sappho* and
two minor pieces, and the addition of *A Farewell*. In a
short preface Arnold qualified the opinions on the choice
of subjects expressed in that of 1853 by an admission that
they might not altogether apply to lyric poetry. In
November he notes that a review in *The Times* had
brought *Empedocles* to the Derby bookstall. But a note in
the publisher's *Catalogue* of November 1854 shows that
by that date the volumes of 1849 and 1852 had both been
withdrawn from circulation. It is not quite clear exactly
when this took place. I have noted the lengthening of the
Switzerland series in 1857 by the addition of the poem *To
Marguerite* or *Isolation*. But in the meantime Arnold had
made a further draft upon his early work in a 'Second
Series' of *Poems*, which appeared in 1855. It at last
restored *Resignation*, together with the *Memorial Verses* on
Wordsworth, *Obermann*, *The Youth of Nature*, *The Youth of
Man*, and *A Summer Night*, and some further extracts from
Empedocles, here entitled *The Harp-Player on Etna*. Some
minor things also reappeared, and, in fact, between
1853 and 1857 very little of the 1849 and 1852 matter

remained derelict. The grouping of the poems on Arnold's courtship as *Faded Leaves*, with the addition of *Separation*, was now introduced. The only other new poem was *Balder Dead*, a blank-verse narrative of over 1,200 lines on a Scandinavian theme. Somebody once called it *Balderdash*. That was not quite fair, but I do not think that it shows Arnold at his best. In 1855 appeared in *Fraser's Magazine* both the elegy on the death of Charlotte Brontë, called *Haworth Churchyard*, and the *Stanzas from the Grande Chartreuse*. These are perhaps too long, but they contain notable passages. In the *Stanzas* Arnold recurs to his favourite image.

> Our fathers watered with their tears
> This sea of time whereon we sail;
> Their voices were in all men's ears
> Who passed within their puissant hail.
> Still the same Ocean round us raves,
> But we stand mute and watch the waves.

In 1856 Arnold wrote to his sister Jane,

My poems are making their way, I think, though slowly, and perhaps never to make way very far. There must always be some people, however, to whom the literalness and sincerity of them has a charm.

In 1857 he had two or three things in hand, which he said he could not finish until he had again breathed and smelt Swiss air.

In 1858, after an interval of three years, he again appeared as a poet, in his tragedy of *Merope*, to which he prefixed an elaborate preface on Greek drama, which he had taken as his model, and on work of the same kind by Goethe, Voltaire, Milton, Pope, and Dryden. It is rather an academic exercise, but he hoped that it would have what Buddha called 'the character of *Fixity*, that true sign of the Law'. He did not, however, perhaps fortunately, intend to proceed farther on the same lines.

But he wrote a good deal to his family and to others in defence of it, and at one time attempted to get Helena Faucit to produce it on the stage. As late as 1865 he still thought there was a certain solidity in its composition, which made it look as well then as five years before. He admitted that the chorus rhythms were unsatisfactory, but could not yet feel that rhyme would do.

Some more magazine work followed in *Men of Genius* and *Saint Brandan*, both of 1860, and in *A Southern Night* of 1861. In the latter year he also attempted some Homeric translations, for use in his lectures, and then, after another long interval, came in 1866 his beautiful *Thyrsis*, the crown of his achievement in verse. *Men of Genius* was dropped, but the other three were included in Arnold's *New Poems* of 1867, his first collected volume since 1853. This has an opening motto.

> Though the Muse be gone away,
> Though she move not earth to-day,
> Souls, erewhile who caught her word,
> Ah! still harp on what they heard.

Empedocles was now restored in full, at the request of Browning. There was a final salvage of five small things from the 1852 volume. But there were also a good many new things, besides the three recent ones just noted. *The Terrace at Berne* has already been considered. *Dover Beach* and *Calais Sands* are both related to *Faded Leaves*. In *Dover Beach* we get a variant of the River of Time motive. The world, says Arnold, is not the land of dreams that we think it.

> And we are here as on a darkling plain
> Swept with confused alarms of struggle and flight,
> Where ignorant armies clash by night.

Other important things are *Rugby Chapel*, written in 1857 on Arnold's father, *Stanzas Composed at Carnac*, on the death of his brother William Delafield in 1859, to which may be added *Bacchanalia*, *Heine's Grave*, *Obermann Once More*, and the *Epilogue to Lessing's Laocoon*. From among smaller pieces one may add *The Last Word* and *A Wish*. In spite of other activities Arnold had still remained a poet during the decade from 1857 to 1867. *New Poems*, he said, was a labour of love. He was pleased when he learned that nearly 1,000 copies had been sold. But there was not much more to come. An American collection of his poems had appeared in 1856, which combined his First and Second Series. How far he was himself concerned with it I do not know. In 1869 he published another of his own, in two volumes, one of Narrative and Elegiac, the other of Dramatic and Lyric poems. It had again a motto.

> What poets feel not, when they make,
> A pleasure in creating,
> The world, in *its* turn, will not take
> Pleasure in contemplating.

He did not consider the arrangement of this edition quite final, and already contemplated another, which did not, however, appear until 1877. Here a number of pieces were segregated under the heading of 'Early Poems'. *Haworth Churchyard*, dropped in 1869, was restored, with an Epilogue. A volume of *Selected Poems* appeared in 1878. An edition of 1881 recovered *The Church of Brou*, and added *New Rome* and *Geist's Grave*, written on a pet dog. Another, of 1885, in three volumes, had *Westminster Abbey*, written on the death of A. P. Stanley, in 1881, and *Poor Mathias*, again on a pet, this time a canary. Both had already been printed in magazines. In March 1886 and again in August 1887 Arnold was asking himself whether he would ever do anything more in poetry. He had in fact written *Kaiser Dead*, on another dog, in April 1887. It was reprinted in 1890 after Arnold's death in a one-volume edition of his *Poetical*

Works, together with *Horatian Echo*, written as early as
1847, but first published in a magazine of 1887. A still
later edition, first published by the Oxford University
Press in 1909, with an Introduction by Sir Arthur
Quiller-Couch, is of great value to scholarship, both
because it reverts to the order in which the poems were
published, and for its notes and elaborate apparatus of
textual variants. One, long promised by Drs. C. B.
Tinker and H. F. Lowry, has never, I believe, appeared,
but their *The Poetry of Matthew Arnold: A Commentary*
(1940) contains much helpful illustrative matter.

Something must be said in conclusion upon Arnold's
general conception of the nature and function of poetry,
as it developed during the period in which it was his
chief channel of utterance. In the days of his correspondence with Clough he was already much occupied
with this problem, but he was then only tentatively feeling his way. He was considering it in the light, not only
of his own achievement, but also of that of his predecessors and contemporaries. In 1847 he was criticizing
Clough's contributions to *Ambarvalia*.

To *solve* the Universe as you try to do is as irritating as
Tennyson's dawdling with its printed shell is fatiguing to me
to witness: and yet I own that to *re-construct* the Universe is
not a satisfactory attempt either—I keep saying, Shakspeare,
Shakspeare, you are as obscure as life is: yet this unsatisfactori-
ness goes against the poetic office in general: for this must I
think certainly be its end.

His admiration of Shakespeare is clear from his sonnet
of 1849, but he thought that if he and Milton had lived
in the atmosphere of modern feeling the style of each
would have been far less curious and exquisite. On the
other hand, he felt in Clough's own poems a deficiency
of the beautiful, which alone was properly poetical. In
1848 or 1849 he had been reading the *Letters* of Keats.

What harm he has done in English Poetry. As Browning is a
man with a moderate gift, passionately desiring movement and

fulness, and obtaining but a confused multitudinousness, so Keats, with a very high gift, is yet also consumed by this desire; and cannot produce the truly living and moving, as his conscience keeps telling him. They will not be patient neither understand that they must begin with an Idea of the World in order not to be prevailed over by the world's multitudinousness.

And he notes the perplexity which Keats, Tennyson, and others of their kind must occasion to young writers. 'Yes and those damned Elizabethan poets generally.' Still in 1849, 'Consider whether you attain the *beautiful*, and whether your product gives *pleasure*, not excites curiosity and reflexion.' And again, 'What is Keats? A style and form seeker, and this with an impetuosity that heightens the effects of his style almost painfully.' And again, 'There are two offices of Poetry—one to add to one's store of thoughts and feelings—another to compose and elevate the mind by a sustained tone, numerous allusions, and a grand style', as Milton does. These are momentary jottings, perhaps not always consistent. In 1852 he still thought that Keats and Shelley were on a false track when they set themselves to reproduce the exuberance of expression, the charm, the richness of images, and the felicity of the Elizabethan poets. Critics still think that the object of poetry is to produce exquisite bits and images. And then comes a passage which is notable, because it anticipates a definition of poetry which Arnold, rightly or wrongly, was to assert later.

Modern poetry can only subsist by becoming a complete *magister vitae*, as the poetry of the ancients did.

In 1853 he was reading Shakespeare's *Tempest*.

How ill he often writes! but how often too how incomparably!

He had not had to grapple with modern theories on the 'disintegration' of Shakespeare.

In his *Preface* to the *Poems* of 1853 Arnold has a good deal to say about poetry, as he then conceived it.

What are the eternal objects of Poetry, among all nations, and at all times? They are actions; human actions; possessing an inherent interest in themselves, and which are to be communicated in an interesting manner by the art of the Poet.

He is here thinking primarily of dramatic poetry. I have already said something about his view of this, and will not repeat it. But he goes on to make a statement of wider range. The modern critic tells the poet that 'a true allegory of the state of one's own mind in a representative history is perhaps the highest thing that one can attempt in the way of poetry'. This Arnold entirely denies. 'No great poetical work has ever been produced with such an aim.' He is asserting—rightly perhaps as regards dramatic poetry, but surely wrongly as regards lyric poetry—the pre-eminence of objectivity over subjectivity. He thinks that Shakespeare's gift of 'happy, abundant, and ingenious expression' has thrown his other excellences into the shade, and furnished a bad model for later poets.

These other excellencies were his fundamental excellencies *as a poet*; what distinguishes the artist from the mere amateur, says Goethe, is *Architectonicè* in the highest sense; that power of execution, which creates, forms, and constitutes: not the profoundness of single thoughts, not the richness of imagery, not the abundance of illustration.

He takes Keats's *Isabella, or the Pot of Basil* as an example of the danger of disregarding this. In his *Epilogue to Lessing's Laocoon* of 1867 he goes back to his *magister vitae* of 1852 and emphasizes the obligation of the poet to trace the progress of life.

> But, ah, then comes his sorest spell
> Of toil! he must life's *movement* tell!
> The thread which binds it all in one,
> And not its separate parts alone!
> The movement he must tell of life,
> Its pain and pleasure, rest and strife;

His eye must travel down, at full,
The long, unpausing spectacle;
With faithful unrelaxing force
Attend it from its primal source,
From change to change and year to year
Attend it of its mid career,
Attend it to the last repose
And solemn silence of its close.

I sometimes think that Arnold, in his prose writings, tends to lay insufficient stress on that element in poetry which consists in the expression, and by expression the communication, of emotion. But here, and in how many other places, the poems themselves make amends for that oversight.

There is no doubt, I think, that Arnold came in time to regard himself as something of a rival to Tennyson as a poet. Posterity must judge. In 1853 he noted a likeness between *Sohrab and Rustum* and the *Morte d'Arthur*, which he thought due to a common imitation of Homer, and later altered a bit in his own poem which he thought 'rather Tennysonian—at any rate not good'. And he quoted some critics who had called it a step in advance of Tennyson in its strain. But he found a difference in the style of the two poems and in their movement. In 1861 Tennyson had apparently asked him through Clough for a volume of his poems. He would send it. 'You need not add that I care for his productions less and less.' In 1862 he noted that Tennyson's lines on the Prince Consort had little poetical value. In 1864 he admired *Enoch Arden*, but did not think Tennyson a great and powerful spirit, like Goethe, Wordsworth, and Byron, in any line. He could not criticize him freely, as it would be attributed to odious motives. In 1869 he wrote to his mother that he thought his own poems represented, on the whole, the main movement of mind of the last quarter of a century.

It might be fairly urged that I have less poetical sentiment than Tennyson, and less intellectual vigour and abundance than Browning; yet, because I have perhaps more of a fusion of the two than either of them, and have more regularly applied that fusion to the main line of modern development, I am likely enough to have my turn, as they have had theirs.

As late as 1880 he noted of Tennyson's *De Profundis*, 'Did you ever?' But the poetical criticism of his closing years must await a later chapter.

V

THE PROFESSOR

ON 5 May 1857 Arnold was elected to the Professorship of Poetry at Oxford, by a majority of eighty-five votes. The income would be about £130 a year. The duties were light, and would not interfere with his school inspection. He was expected to assist in looking over prize compositions, to deliver a Latin oration in praise of founders at every alternate Commemoration, and to give three Latin lectures on ancient poetry each year. But for these he was allowed to substitute English ones. He was pleased that Keble, apparently after some hesitation, voted for him. He welcomed the appointment, because it brought him once more in touch with Oxford. In 1854 he had written,

I am much struck with the apathy and *poorness* of the people here, as they now strike me, and their petty pottering habits as compared with the students of Paris, or Germany, or even of London. Animation and interest and the power of work seem so sadly wanting in them. And I think this is so; and the place, in losing Newman and his followers, has lost its religious movement, which after all kept it from stagnating, and has not yet, so far as I see, got anything better. However, we must hope that the coming changes, and perhaps the infusion of Dissenters' sons of that muscular, hard-working *unblasé* middle class—for it is this, in spite of its abominable disagreeableness—may brace the flaccid sinews of Oxford a little.

Nevertheless he now confided to his brother Tom,

I am hardly ever at Oxford now, but the sentiment of the place is overpowering to me when I have leisure time to feel it, and can shake off the interruptions which it is not so easy to shake off now as it was when we were young.

His inaugural lecture, given in the autumn of 1857, was *On the Modern Element in Literature*. He declared it the duty of a teacher, himself delivered and consoled by study, to help others on their way to a similar result. Not only a moral, but also an intellectual deliverance is needed. It is 'the peculiar demand of those ages which are called modern'. He will attempt to show that even for modern times the literature of ancient Greece is a mighty engine of intellectual deliverance. The present age gives the spectacle of a vast multitude of facts awaiting and inviting comprehension. It has a copious and complex present and behind it a copious and complex past. The deliverance consists in man's comprehension of these. He who has found the point of view from which to contemplate the spectacle, and interprets it to his age, is one of his age's intellectual deliverers. The spectacle is immense. It is the collective life of humanity. All the elements of our spectacle are not of equal value. The most interesting literatures are those which have most successfully solved for their ages the problem which occupies ours. He is already on the lines of his definition of literature as a 'criticism of life', although he did not formulate it until later. It is to the poetical literature of an age, he thinks, that we must, in general, look for the most perfect, the most adequate, representation of that age.

He turns to Athens in the fifth century B.C., the age of Pericles, as a great literary epoch. The account by Thucydides of the Peloponnesian War is more 'modern' in spirit than Raleigh's *History of the World*. Pindar, Aeschylus, Sophocles, even Aristophanes, on the comic side, are 'adequate' in his sense of the term. Homer is eternally interesting, but his age is less interesting than himself. In the Roman world Lucretius is modern, but is he 'adequate'? Virgil, though the most beautiful and attractive figure in literary history, is not an adequate interpreter of his age. And if Lucretius and Virgil lack cheerfulness, Horace wants seriousness.

A preface to this lecture, when it was printed in 1869,

notes that it was meant to be followed and completed by a course of lectures developing the subject entirely, and some of these were given. But the course was broken off because Arnold found his knowledge insufficient for treating in a solid way many portions of the subject chosen. In January 1858, William Wordsworth, the younger, wrote to Henry Crabb Robinson on the inaugural lecture:

As a composition it was pointed and telling: tho' the matter was little to my taste: he seems to lust after a system of his own: and systems are not made in a day: or if they are—like a hastily-built fort, the stronger they are at one point, so much the weaker are they at another.

I do not know that this opinion is of any great value.

The subjects of the lectures in 1858 are unknown. One of those in 1859 was probably on the Troubadours, and the other may have been on Dante. An article on *Dante and Beatrice* in *Fraser's Magazine* during 1863 is rather short, but he wrote of it as an old lecture. Probably, however, he often revised what he had spoken before it got into print. In December 1859 he contemplated giving five lectures by the end of 1860 and then publishing them. The first would include an examination of the origin of the 'romantic sentiment about women', in connexion with which he had been reading an essay by Ernest Renan on Celtic poetry. It may have been given early in 1860, but if so it is lost. In fact he accomplished at most three lectures, instead of his usual two, during that year. In October he was working at one on Homer. He called it an 'off lecture' and said that he should continue his proper course towards the end of term. Whatever he now considered his 'proper course' to be, this second autumn lecture was also on Homer, and so was another given in January 1861. More precisely, the title of the three, when they came to be printed later in the year, was *On Translating Homer*. I can, of course, only briefly summarize his points. There is naturally much about

Homer himself. He is rapid, plain, and direct, both in his words and syntax, and in the substance of his thought. Above all, he is eminently noble. By neglecting one or more of these qualities, most of his translators have failed. Cowper, Wright, Pope, Sotheby, and Chapman are in turn condemned. The latest, Francis William Newman, a brother of the Cardinal, whom Arnold had once seen in his house and written down 'an hass', has done worse than any of them through his inability to reproduce Homer's nobility. He thought he ought to be quaint, but not grotesque. He ought not to have been either, said Arnold, but was grotesque. In a comparison by Newman of Homer with old English balladry he found a little truth, but exaggerated. Even Scott's ballad poetry, fine as it was, he thought not in Homer's style, or in the grand style which Virgil, Dante, and Milton shared with him. But the grandeur of Milton's verse was one thing, that of Homer's another. Homer's, he repeats, was flowing and rapid, but Milton's was laboured and self-retarding. On the other hand 'the noble and profound application of ideas to life', which Homer shared with Milton, he thought 'the most essential part of poetic greatness'. As to metres, he did not think either blank verse or disyllabic couplets suitable for rendering Homer. He suggested the use of the English hexameter, and attempted some examples of his own in this form. In the course of these lectures he recurs to his theme of the eccentricity and arbitrariness which he finds in the English writers of his own day, just as much as in their Elizabethan predecessors. English literature he now ranks after those of France and Germany. The main effort there for many years has been a *critical* effort, the endeavour, in all branches of knowledge, theology, philosophy, history, art, science, to see the object as in itself it really is. But almost the last thing for which one would come to English literature is just that very thing which now Europe most desires—*criticism*.

Arnold wrote to his sister Jane at the end of January 1861 that at the end of his third Homer lecture he was cheered by the audience, which was very uncommon at Oxford. The lectures themselves would reach her in a day or two. They were printed, not in magazines, but in volume form. About a fortnight later he added:

So you find my tone in the Lectures too dogmatic? I shall be curious to see if the reviewers find the same thing. The tone of a lecturing professor to an audience, supposed to be there to learn of him, cannot be quite that of a man submitting his views to the great world. The expression to speak *ex cathedra* in itself implies what is expected in one who speaks from a Professor's chair.

By the middle of March he was expecting an attack on him in the *Saturday Review*. It came at the end of July, in an article on *Homeric Translators and Critics*. I think, though I am not certain, that the author was James Spedding. It only gave Arnold temporary annoyance. More troublesome was a rather portentous onslaught by Francis Newman in *Homeric Translation in Theory and Practice: A Reply to Matthew Arnold Esq.* An answer to this was almost inevitable. Arnold took his time about it. The subject of his second lecture in 1861, if there was one, is not known. But by November he was ready to begin his *Last Words on Homer*, which was finished by March 1862, and became his first lecture for that year. He was told that everyone thought it 'perfect in tone and convincingness'. He had been courteous in it to his opponent, while still maintaining his own views on the points at issue between them. The four lectures were later combined in a single volume.

In June 1862 Arnold had to give the Latin Creweian Oration at the Encaenia. It was a responsibility which fell in alternate years to the Professor and the Public Orator. The subject of his second lecture for this year, if there was one, is uncertain. It may have been the essay on Maurice de Guérin, printed in January 1863. Here he notes the interpretative power of poetry, which deals with things so as to awaken in us a wonderfully full, new, and intimate sense of them and of our relations with them. In February 1863 he had a heavy programme before him. He expected to print before the summer not less than six articles, on Spinoza, Dante, Marcus Aurelius, A French Eton, Academies, Eugénie de Guérin, and perhaps a seventh on Joubert. And in addition to these he must write two lectures. After the summer he meant to lie fallow for some time, or to busy himself with poetry only. His first lecture during that year was on *Heinrich Heine*. Here he first introduces a term, borrowed from German writers, of which he was to make frequent use later.

Philistinism!—we have not the expression in English. Perhaps we have not the word because we have so much of the thing. Philistine must have originally meant, in the minds of those who invented the nickname, a strong, dogged unenlightened opponent of the chosen people, of the children of the light.

In a letter to his mother he said:

I have almost always a very fair attendance; to be sure it is chiefly composed of ladies. But I am obliged always to think, in composing my lectures, of the public who will read me, not of the dead bones who will hear me, or my spirit would fail.

The contemplated article on *Joseph Joubert* became, in fact, his second lecture of 1863. It is here that he arrives at his final definition of literature, including, of course, poetry, as 'a criticism of life'. Its end and aim, he says, if one considers it attentively, is nothing but that. 'A criticism of life' is not very different from his *magister vitae* of 1852. But it links with the importance which Arnold, now on the road to becoming a philosopher, was to attach to 'criticism' as a factor in his survey of English social life in general, and in particular that of the middle classes. He compares Joubert favourably with

both Coleridge and Macaulay as a thinker, though he
finds value in Coleridge too, in spite of many reserva-
tions. In this lecture, too, the Philistines more than once
make their appearance. Perhaps both Heine and Joubert
were rather outside the range of reading to be expected
of a normal Oxford undergraduate. A journalistic
article on Arnold, entitled *The Critical Character*, led him
to say:

> It contains so much praise that you must have thought I
> wrote it myself, except that I should hardly have called myself
> by the hideous title of 'Professor'.

Later in 1863 or early in 1864, he reverts to Joubert as
'a moralist really of the first order, really at the centre by
his ideas' in the course of an article, which he had for
some time been contemplating, on *The Literary Influence of
Academies*. He is not thinking of schools, but of associations
of men of letters such as the French Academy founded in
1629, with the encouragement of Cardinal Richelieu, to
be a literary tribunal, reviewing the work of authors, and,
if it thought fit, approving the publication of it. He notes
the French conscience in intellectual matters, which we
do not share. The spiritual characteristics of our nation
are energy and honesty, not an open and clear mind, not
a quick and flexible intelligence. Genius and energy
have given us Shakespeare and Newton. Energy de-
mands freedom, and a nation which has it will not be apt
to set up a fixed standard, an authority, like an Academy.
But some of the requisites of intellectual work are specially
the affair of quickness of mind and flexibility of intelligence. These qualities, though important, are secondary
in poetry and energy is the first thing, but in prose they
are of first-rate importance. Academies consecrate and
maintain them. Our nation is greater in poetry than
prose. With Frenchmen it is the reverse. Our journey-
man work is less well done than theirs, for which the
Academy serves as a centre and rallying-point. The

urbanity of Cardinal Newman is a quality rare in this country. In the absence of an Academy a note of provinciality is observable. It is often so with Burke, who often writes extravagant prose. It is 'Asiatic' prose. Kinglake's is 'Corinthian', Addison's is 'Attic', but the note of provinciality comes in the commonplace of his ideas. How different is Ruskin when he is exercising his genius, and when he is exercising his intelligence! Palgrave has a fine critical tact, but it is marred by freaks and violences. The article is particularly interesting, because Arnold is here largely criticizing his contemporaries. On the whole Arnold thinks that it would not be wise to establish an Academy on the French model now. It is too late for our literature to abandon its traditions. But let us remember to widen our culture, and remember that mere glorification of ourselves or our literature is both vulgar and retarding. Later it was asserted that he wanted an Academy in England. He denied it. He knew what it would be like—a happy family of everything which is influential, accomplished, and distinguished; and then, some fine morning, a dissatisfaction of the public mind with this brilliant and select coterie, a flight of Corinthian leading articles, and an irruption of Mr. G. A. Sala.

Arnold's first lecture of 1864 was on *Pagan and Christian Religious Sentiment*, which was printed in the *Cornhill*, with a good deal about Protestantism left out, as it could not be stated fully enough to explain and secure itself. This was a topic on which he was to have much to say later. His second lecture was probably on *The Function of Criticism at the Present Time*. Here he deals with some rejoinders to his statement in the Homer lectures, which I have cited above, that in France and Germany, but not in England, there had now been for many years a critical effort 'to see the object as in itself it really is'. The rejoinders had asserted 'the inherent superiority of the creative effort of the human spirit over its critical effort'.

He admits that the critical power is of lower rank than the creative. The exercise of a creative power is the highest function of man. But he may have the sense of exercising it, not only in producing great works of literature, but also in well-doing, in learning, even in criticizing. And the creative power must have materials to work on. In literature these are ideas, 'the best ideas on every matter which literature touches, current at the time'. They are not in its own control, but more within that of the critical power, the business of which is, once more, 'to see the object as in itself it really is'. Goethe had this power. The English poetry of the early nineteenth century, especially Byron's, but also Shelley's, and even Wordsworth's, lacked it. In the Greece of Pindar and Sophocles, in the England of Shakespeare, the poet lived in a current of ideas, animating and nourishing to the creative power. Goethe had a sort of equivalent in the complete culture and unfettered thinking of a large body of Germans. England in the first quarter of the nineteenth century had neither of these advantages. The French Revolution had ideas, but suffered from the mania for giving an immediate and practical application to them. Burke is great, because he brought thought to bear on politics. The Englishman values what is political and practical, and the notion of the free play of the mind upon all subjects being an object of desire hardly enters into his thoughts. Possibly now, in peace, the ideas of Europe may steal gradually in, and may lead in the end to an apparition of intellectual life. It is merely the privilege of faith at present to discern this end. We must look for criticism first, then perhaps a time of true creative activity. The rule of criticism must be 'disinterestedness', in following the law of its own nature, which is to be 'a free play of mind on all subjects which it touches'. Its business is 'simply to know the best that is known and thought in the world'.

He turns to a survey of current English criticism, as he

finds it in organs such as the *Edinburgh Review*, the *Quarterly Review*, the *British Quarterly Review*, and *The Times*. They are organs of men and parties with practical ends to serve, and just so much play of mind as may suit their being that. The dithyrambs they print on 'the old Anglo-Saxon race, the best breed in the whole world' are curiously inconsistent with some of the grim facts of our civilization which they record. The action which he is himself proposing for criticism is a very subtle and indirect one. The mass of mankind will never have any ardent zeal for seeing things as they are. Very inadequate ideas will always satisfy them. Whoever sets himself to see things as they are will find himself one of a very small circle; but it is only by this small circle resolutely doing its own work that adequate ideas will ever get current at all. The practical man is not apt for fine distinctions. How can Cobbett, Carlyle, and Ruskin not be misunderstood if they tell the political Englishman that our august constitution sometimes looks like a colossal machine for the manufacture of Philistines? Arnold will have much more to say about Philistines later. The political man will say 'Let us have a party' and call it *The Liberal Party*, and back each other up, with no nonsense about independent criticism and intellectual delicacy, and no trouble about foreign thought. But the critic is not to go with the stream. He must resist, and if in vain, cry with Obermann, *Périssons en résistant*. Criticism must maintain its independence of the practical spirit and its aims. There is a lull among reformers now, which he does not regret. We have got all that can be got by seeing everything in connexion with politics and practical life. Let us try a more disinterested mode of seeing them. Let us betake ourselves more to the serener life of the mind and spirit. The idea of a disinterested endeavour to learn and propagate the best that is known and thought in the world obliges the English critic to dwell much on foreign thought. He will be told that he is expected to address himself to

English critics and criticism. He is sorry, but little current English literature comes within the definition he has just given. He will conclude as he began. To have the sense of creative activity is the great happiness and the great proof of being alive, and it is not denied to criticism to know it. But then criticism must be sincere, simple, flexible, ardent, ever widening in knowledge. Then it may have, in no contemptible measure, a joyful sense of creative activity. He admits that, in full measure, the sense of creative activity belongs only to genuine creation. But what man of letters can ever forget that? The epochs of Aeschylus and Shakespeare make us feel their pre-eminence. That promised land it will not be ours to attain, and we shall die in the wilderness. But to have desired to enter it, to have saluted it from afar, is already, perhaps, the best distinction among contemporaries; it will certainly be the best title to esteem with posterity. It is a notable utterance. Arnold is, of course, again giving a wider sense to the term 'criticism' than that of the mere appreciation of literary merit.

He had again controversy to face. *The Function of Criticism* was printed in the *National Review* for November 1864, and in December came a long attack on it in the *Saturday Review* by James Fitzjames Stephen, which was entitled *Mr. Matthew Arnold and his Countrymen.* He claimed that Arnold had formed an unjust estimate of his contemporaries, and condemned the indecency of talking about 'British Philistines'. He asserted that Arnold too readily assumed the truth of the transcendental system of philosophy. The English were a practical people, and some at least of their philosophers had rejected that system. He had not meant to be discourteous to Arnold personally, and sent his wife to call, in token of amity. Arnold's rejoinder was delayed by an educational mission abroad, which occupied him during the April to October of 1865. It appeared, however, in the *Cornhill Magazine* for February 1866, with the title of

My Countrymen. He knew well, he said, that the heart of the English nation was in the middle class, and cited the glorification of this by certain writers, who thought it characterized not by Philistinism, but by enlightenment. He had not, in his recent travels, found foreign opinion sharing this view. He admits, in irony, that foreigners envy us, and that this warps their judgement, and goes on, in the same vein, with searching criticism of the English middle class and its Parliamentary spokesmen. He admits that a large number of the more well-to-do members of that class get as good an education as the aristocrats, but even they are too much influenced by the aristocrats themselves to show real intelligence. This article was answered by a woman calling herself Horace, in the *Pall Mall Gazette,* and in March Arnold reasserted his views in *A Courteous Explanation,* which he said he wrote from Grub Street.

But I am anticipating. In the summer of 1864, Arnold, as Professor, had the task of reading all the Oxford prize compositions for the year. Terrible work he found it, 'worse even than writing one's rubbish'. Early in 1865 he collected much of his recent work in a volume of *Essays in Criticism.* In the foreground stood *The Function of Criticism.* There were three other lectures, those on *Heine, Joubert,* and *Pagan and Mediaeval Religious Sentiment,* and five articles, contributed to periodicals, on *The Literary Influence of Academies, Maurice de Guérin, Eugénie de Guérin, Marcus Aurelius,* and *Spinoza.* When it first appeared in *Macmillan's Magazine* for December 1863, *Spinoza* had been called *A Word more about Spinoza.* In a second edition (1869) of the essays it was conflated with *The Bishop and the Philosopher,* which had also been in *Macmillan's* for January 1863, and the title was altered to *Spinoza and the Bible.* In a third edition of 1875 *A Persian Passion Play,* originally a lecture of 1871 at Birmingham, was added. To the original edition of 1865 Arnold prefixed a *Preface,* which he thought would make his mother laugh.

When he read it to a brother and sister, they received
it in such solemn silence, that he began to tremble.
Evidently there were some indiscretions in it, which were
removed later. As the *Preface* now stands, there is a little
more about the onslaughts against his *Homer* and *The
Function of Criticism*, and a beautiful passage on Oxford.
I will give it a paragraph to itself.

Beautiful city! so venerable, so lovely, so unravaged by the
fierce intellectual life of our century, so serene!

There are our young barbarians, all at play! And yet,
steeped in sentiment as she lies, spreading her gardens to the
moonlight, and whispering from her towers the last enchant-
ments of the Middle Age, who will deny that Oxford, by her
ineffable charm, keeps ever calling us nearer to the true goal
of all of us, to the ideal, to perfection,—to beauty, in a word,
which is only truth seen from another side?—nearer, perhaps,
than all the science of Tübingen. Adorable dreamer, whose
heart has been so romantic! who hast given thyself so prodigally,
given thyself to sides and to heroes not mine, only never to the
Philistines! home of lost causes, and forsaken beliefs, and unpopular names, and impossible loyalties! what example could
ever so inspire us to keep down the Philistine in ourselves, what
teacher could ever so save us from that bondage to which we
are all prone. . . . She will forgive me, even if I have unwittingly
drawn upon her a shot or two aimed at her unworthy son; for
she is generous, and the cause in which I fight is, after all, hers.
Apparitions of a dog, what is our puny warfare against the
Philistines, compared with the warfare which this queen of
romance has been waging against them for centuries, and will
wage after we are gone?

This is Arnold at his best.

In March and April 1865 he was working at a lecture,
and in September he said he was in arrear at Oxford and
getting fined. I do not quite know why. He had been
delayed by a journey abroad for the Education Office,
but a series of four lectures seems to have come quite
regularly in 1865 and 1866. It was on *Celtic Literature*,
a subject which he did not find suited for 'show-lectures'.

In fact he knew nothing of Celtic tongues, and this series is rather below his usual standard. Nevertheless, when he ended the last, the old Principal of Jesus College said audibly, 'The Angel ended'. He was plagued with his Latin speech at the Encaenia of 1866, 'that absurd scene', but hoped that a Professorship of Celtic might be established in Oxford. His last lecture there was in the summer of 1867. The subject was *Culture and its Enemies*, but what he had here to say will be best discussed in the next chapter. He tried to make this last utterance one in which he could keep to ground where he was in sympathy with Oxford, having often enough startled it with heresies and novelties, and he thought he had succeeded.

Perhaps none but Oxford men can know how much truth there really is in the praise I have given to Oxford for her sentiment.

He would have liked Robert Browning to succeed him as Professor, but it was an obstacle that Browning had no academic degree. It was perhaps a reminiscence of his lectures which led him to say to George Russell, in the last year of his life:

People think I can teach them style. What stuff it all is! Have something to say, and say it as clearly as you can. That is the only secret of style.

THE PHILOSOPHER

IN the foregoing chapters I have noted many indications which suggested that it was Arnold's destiny to become in middle life a philosopher and in particular a social philosopher, rather than a student of belles-lettres. In his youthful days he had been influenced by Goethe, Froude, perhaps Emerson, and Carlyle, although of Carlyle he became doubtful. He called him 'restful' in 1848, but in 1849 a 'moral desperado'. In 1847 he refused to solve the Universe. That is no doubt beyond any of us. It is perhaps an easier task to solve the problem of man's life upon earth, and to that he was early drawn. His first approaches were naturally tentative. In 1848 he was reading Obermann. In the same year, discussing the French Revolution he observed that, after all man's shifting of postures, *'restat vivere'*. A little later he noted the need to 'begin with an Idea of the world in order not to be prevailed over by the world's multitudinousness'. His sonnets of 1849 praise Sophocles,

> who saw life steadily and saw it whole,

and the wit of Wellington,

> which saw *one* clue to life and follow'd it.

In other poems, over a good many years, there is the constant theme of the River of Life, or of Time. Was it in his mind that, although you cannot stop the flow of a river, you can divert it and make it productive? In 1852 he declared that poetry can only subsist by becoming a *'magister vitae'*. In 1857 he hoped that his *Merope* would have what Buddha called the 'character of *Fixity*, that true sign of the Law'. In his inaugural lecture of the same year he declared the man who could contemplate the collective life of humanity, and interpret it to his age, was one of that age's intellectual deliverers. In 1863 came his famous definition of literature as a 'criticism of life'. I will add one other point here. It was his habit to set up annually a *Note Book* in which he kept a record of things read and to be read during the year, together with occasional notes for his own literary and spiritual guidance. In several of these, from 1857 onwards, which have been published, occurs the notable maxim

Semper aliquid certi proponendum est.

This is just Buddha's *Fixity* again.

More than once, during the period of his Professorship, Arnold turned aside from his lectures to write magazine articles on subjects not directly related to them. Two at least of these were on religion, again a topic on which he was destined to say much later. In 1861 J. W. Colenso, the Bishop of Natal, had written a treatise on St. Paul's *Epistle to the Romans*, which was thought heretical. In 1862 and 1863 he followed this up with another on the *Pentateuch*, which he declared to be a document of a very much later date than that traditionally ascribed to it. With the trouble into which this brought Colenso with his ecclesiastical superiors we need not concern ourselves. But he certainly fluttered the religious dovecotes of England. F. D. Maurice, himself a Broad Churchman, was one of those alarmed. Colenso was criticized during 1863 by Arthur Stanley in the first instalment of his *History of the Jewish Church*, but without any attempt to insist on the literal inspiration of every word and letter of the Bible. Arnold was much interested in the controversy. He approached it largely from the angle of Benedictus Spinoza, a philosopher of the seventeenth century, in whom he had long been interested. As far back as 1849 or 1850 he had written to Clough of 'the positive and vivifying atmosphere' of Spinoza, and added:

This last, smile as you will, I have been studying lately with profit.

There are some other allusions to Spinoza in later letters to Clough. And now in November 1862 he told his mother that he was going to write an article called *The Bishop and the Philosopher*, in which he should contrast Colenso's jejune and technical manner of dealing with Biblical controversy with the edifying and pious spirit of Spinoza in his *Interpretation of Scripture*. This article appeared in *Macmillan's Magazine* for January 1863, and he was pleased with it. There were rejoinders, one in the *Spectator* by an anonymous writer, with the title of *Mr. Matthew Arnold and the Aristocratic Creed*, another by F. D. Maurice, with that of *Spinoza and Professor Arnold*. In *Macmillan's Magazine* for February 1863 Arnold reviewed Stanley's *History*. His conclusions here may be briefly summarized. Spinoza says that the Bible contains much that is mere history, and, like all history, sometimes true, sometimes false. He uttered it not as a religious teacher, but as an independent philosopher. Colenso, on the other hand, does speak as a religious teacher to the religious world. He takes the proposition, 'Every letter in the Bible is the direct utterance of the Most High', and, while denying it, exaggerates the importance of his denial by not allowing the reader to recollect that the religious life is wholly independent of this idea. Stanley, shutting his mind against no ideas brought by the spirit of his time, sets these ideas, in the sphere of the religious life, in their right prominence, and still puts that first which is first. He keeps the centre of the religious life where it should be. He gives a lesson not only to the Bishop of Natal, but also to the Bishop's adversaries, who repeat the Bishop's error in giving undue prominence to certain intellectual propositions, on which the essence and vitality of the religious life in no way depends. In February 1863 Arnold was contemplating another article on Spinoza for *The Times*. Perhaps it was not accepted, for in November he told his mother that he was not satisfied with his *Times* Spinoza, as an article for *Macmillan's*, and

his *A Word more about Spinoza* appeared in *Macmillan's* for
the following December. In his lecture during 1864 on
The Function of Criticism he referred to the storm which his
handling of Colenso had aroused. Here was a liberal
attacking a liberal. In a note to this lecture, as it appears
in the 1869 edition of his *Essays in Criticism*, he says that,
in view of his dislike of personal attack and controversy,
he now abstained from reprinting his articles on the
Bishop's book. He was, however, sincerely impenitent
for having published them, and repeated his original
remark:

There is truth of science and truth of religion; truth of science
does not become truth of religion till it is made religious.

In the same edition of the *Essays* is a long article on
Spinoza and the Bible which does not refer to Colenso.
Apparently it is based on *A Word more about Spinoza*,
but also contains some salvage from *The Bishop and the
Philosopher*.

But if Arnold, in the intervals of his lectures, largely
occupied himself with religion, he had not altogether
forgotten social civilization. This, however, he was
inclined to handle for a time in a lighter mood. During
1866–7 he wrote several letters to the *Pall Mall Gazette*
in which he professed to state not his own views, but those
of one Arminius von Thunder-ten-Tronckh, a German
whom he had met abroad and who occasionally visited
England. The letters are extremely amusing, and dis-
close a lighter vein in him than we might sometimes suppose. Arminius comments on the lack of intelligence,
which he calls *Geist*, in our classes, and especially the
middle class. There is much about the Philistines. Of
these there are three varieties, the religious Philistine, the
well-to-do Philistine, and the rowdy Philistine. Arminius
contrasts their mental attitudes with the culture and
avoidance of clap-trap which he claimed to be characteristic of his own Germany. He sees a bench of magistrates,

Lord Lumpington, a peer, Esau Hittall, a clergyman,
Mr. Bottles, a self-made middle-class man, and comments
ironically on the types of education which were supposed
to have fitted them for their job. Arnold, in reply, spoke
of the 'incomparable and truly British qualities' which
had just given us the Atlantic telegraph. 'Pshaw,' said
Arminius, 'that great rope, with a Philistine at each end
of it talking inutilities.' And so on. In 1869 the letters
were resumed, in the light of a Bill for allowing a man to
marry his deceased wife's sister. Arnold collected the
whole series in his *Friendship's Garland* of 1871. One other
isolated writing of 1861 must also be noted. This was an
essay on *Democracy*, originally written as a Preface to
Arnold's *Report* on his educational mission abroad in
1859. Here he notes the doctrine of English aristocracy
and the growing attempt of the classes to assert themselves in a demand for social rather than political freedom. They wanted 'equality'. Of this he had found
much more in France. He thinks the incapacity of
aristocracies for ideas had led to a loss of sympathy with
the instinct of the masses for expansion and a fuller life.
There had been some recent advance in culture among
all classes, but the superiority of the higher class in that
was becoming less obvious. Character without culture
he thought raw, blind, and dangerous, and culture without character frivolous, vain, and weak. He wanted
state action to provide better schools for the middle
classes, in order to improve their culture.

This emphasis on culture brings us back to his last
lecture of 8 June 1867, on *Culture and its Enemies*. This
was printed in the *Cornhill* for July 1867. In a letter to the
Pall Mall Gazette of the previous April he had referred,
jestingly, to a growing Jacobinical spirit, which had
given him alarm, and declared that he had seen 'that
powerful young publicist, Mr. Frederic Harrison, furbish-
ing up a guillotine'. In the lecture he returned to
Harrison, citing some utterance unknown to me. He

classed him with other liberals who called culture a
'frivolous and useless thing'. That he thought natural,
since culture eternally opposed the two signal marks of
Jacobinism, its fierceness and its addiction to an abstract
system. Harrison had declared, 'The man of culture
in politics is one of the poorest mortals alive', and had
asked what the use of culture was, except for a critic of
new books or a professor of belles-lettres. That had
naturally stung Arnold. In the whole of Harrison's
article he found a 'fierce exasperation'. He admits that
preachers of culture are likely to have a rough task in this
country. They are likely long to be regarded as elegant
or spurious Jeremiahs. Later he noted that he had himself been described as an 'elegant Jeremiah' by a writer
in the *Daily Telegraph*, although Jeremiah was the very
one of the Hebrew prophets whose style he admired the
least. When the *Culture* lecture appeared in print,
Harrison was moved to a retort, which he called *Culture,
A Dialogue*. It appeared in the *Fortnightly* for November
1867, and is reprinted in the writer's *The Choice of Books*
(1886). It took the form of a witty parody of Arnold's own
conversations with Arminius von Thunder-ten-Tronck in
the *Pall Mall Gazette*. There is much chaff about culture,
the Philistines, and 'sweetness and light'. Has his inter-
locutor, asks Arminius, a systematic social philosophy,
with coherent principles, interdependent, subordinate,
and derivative? But no answer was forthcoming, beyond
a bland smile. Arnold was delighted. 'It is scarcely the
least vicious', he wrote to a friend, 'and in parts so
amusing that I laughed till I cried.' He decided to
answer Harrison and others, who had given him 'golden
opportunities', in a pendant to *Culture and its Enemies*, to
be called *Anarchy and Authority*. Five successive instal-
ments of this appeared, also in the *Cornhill*, from January
to August 1868. In one of them Arnold invented the term
'Barbarians', as a description of the aristocratic class.
This, he told his mother, he thought would stick. He had

some further criticism to meet from Robert Buchanan, 'a clever, but raw and intemperate Scottish youth', who tilted against him in the *Spectator*. In January 1869 he reprinted both the lecture and the magazine articles in book form, under the title of *Culture and Anarchy*, revising then, apparently, the final chapter, which now deals with current legislative proposals for the disestablishment of the Irish Church, and the legitimation of marriage between a man and his deceased wife's sister. This second topic he also considered in a letter to the *Pall Mall Gazette* of June 1869, which is reprinted in *Friendship's Garland*. Here the Bottles family recur. The volume of 1869 had an elaborate Preface, a short Introduction, and a long Conclusion. In the Introduction he refers again to Harrison and his criticism of 'the cant about culture', and also to John Bright, who had said that people who talked about culture meant 'a smattering of the two dead languages of Greek and Latin'. He admits that at the present time men of culture are just the beings who cannot properly be entrusted with power, but is inclined to think that this is the fault of the community, rather than the men of culture themselves.

As *Culture and Anarchy* stands in its final form, it consists of six chapters, entitled respectively, 'Sweetness and Light', which represents the original lecture, 'Doing as one likes', 'Barbarians, Philistines, Populace', 'Hebraism and Hellenism', 'Porro Unum est Necessarium', and 'Our Liberal Practitioners'. Culture played so important a part in Arnold's social philosophy that some analysis of the conception which he had formed of it in 1869 is desirable. It can only be very summary. Much interesting detail of his long argument I must omit. And he would not be Arnold if he did not sometimes repeat himself. The motive of culture, he begins, is not merely curiosity, as its disparagers say. Or, rather, it is not curiosity in the English sense of the term, which always conveys a notion of frivolous and unedifying activity.

It has a better one abroad. There is a curiosity about
intellectual matters which is futile and merely a disease.
But there is another, which is a desire after the things of
the mind simply for their own sakes and for the pleasure
of seeing them as they are. This, in an intelligent being,
is natural and laudable. And there is a wider view still,
in which all the love of our neighbour, the impulses
towards action, help, and beneficence, the desire for
removing human error, clearing human confusion, and
diminishing human misery, the noble aspiration to
leave the world better and happier than we found it—
all these come in as part of the grounds of culture, and
the main and pre-eminent part. Culture then is properly
described as 'a study of perfection'. Bishop Wilson gives
it a motto, 'To make reason and the will of God prevail'.
There are new lights in the world now. The iron force
of adhesion to the old social, political, and religious
routine, of exclusion of all which is new, has wonderfully
yielded. Now is the moment for culture to be of service,
culture which believes in making reason and the will of
God prevail, and in the study of perfection. But perfection is a harmonious expansion of *all* the powers which
make the beauty and worth of human nature, and is not
consistent with the over-development of any one power
at the expense of the rest. Here culture goes beyond
religion, as religion is generally conceived by us. It has
a rough task to achieve in this country. The idea of
perfection as a *harmonious* expansion of human nature is
at variance with our want of flexibility, with our inapti-
tude for seeing more than one side of a thing, with our
intense energetic absorption in the particular pursuit
we happen to be following. Faith in machinery is our
special danger. Another is the argument, 'May not every
man in England say what he likes?' But the aspirations
of culture are not satisfied, unless what men like to say
has good in it, and more good than bad. Englishmen
think that our greatness and welfare are proved by our

being so very rich. But they are just the very people whom we call Philistines. For culture, wealth is nothing but machinery. So, too, are population and bodily health and vigour, on which Englishmen lay such stress. He cites Epictetus, who called it a sign of ἀφυΐα, which is a nature not finely tempered, to give yourself up to things which relate to the body. The contrary εὐφυΐα gives exactly the notion of perfection as culture conceives it, a perfection in which the characters of beauty and intelligence are both present. Swift calls them 'the two noblest of things, *sweetness and light*'. Here culture is of like spirit with poetry. Puritanism has its virtues, but also its faults. You do not get sweetness and light in the *Nonconformist's* motto of 'The Dissidence of Dissent and the Protestantism of the Protestant religion'. Culture is not fanatical, even against the 'machinery'. It is flexible enough to see that such a tendency may be necessary as a preparation for something more salutary in the future. Oxford, with its beauty and sweetness, has been in isolation. He is all in its faith and tradition. But Cardinal Newman's movement was broken by middle-class Liberalism. But now this great force of Philistinism is being broken by a more democratic one, which has still its main tendencies to form. It needs the idea of perfection which culture supplies. Some of its friends tend to lead it in the fierce ways of Jacobinism. Culture resists that. It looks beyond machinery and hates hatred. It seeks to do away with classes; to make the best that has been known and thought in the world current everywhere; to make all men live in an atmosphere of sweetness and light, where they may use ideas, as it uses them itself, freely—nourished, and not bound by them. This is the *social idea*; and the men of culture are the true apostles of equality.

So far the original lecture, perhaps after some revision. The remaining chapters contain corollaries and, as already indicated, some repetitions. In *Doing as one likes*, Arnold notes Frederic Harrison's 'good-tempered and witty satire', and some other criticisms, from which he will try to profit. John Bright had declared that the central idea of English life and politics is the assertion of personal liberty. Quite so; but as feudalism with its ideas and habits of subordination dies out, and we are left with nothing but this idea and our system of checks, we are in danger of drifting towards anarchy. We have not the notion, so familiar on the Continent and to antiquity, of the *State* as an organ controlling individual wills in the name of an interest wider than that of individuals. We have our aristocracy, our middle class, and our working class, this last no longer restrained by the strong feudal habits of subordination and deference. All over the country men are beginning to assert and put in practice an Englishman's right to do what he likes—to march where he likes, meet where he likes, enter where he likes, hoot as he likes, threaten as he likes, smash as he likes. All this tends to anarchy. He gives examples. Culture tells us that there is nothing so very blessed in merely doing what one likes, and that the really blessed thing is to like what right reason ordains, and to follow her authority. How are we to get a *State* capable of summing up the right reason of the community, and exercising authority in accordance with it? He discusses various claims that state power should rest with the aristocracy, the middle class, and the lower class respectively, and considers their qualifications to exercise it. Can we then rise to the idea of the whole community, the *State*, and find our centre of light and authority there? We do not, because we habitually live in our ordinary selves which do not carry us beyond the ideas and wishes of the class to which we happen to belong. It is only to our *best self* that we can turn with sure trust. But this is the very self which culture, or the study of perfection, seeks to develop in us. It is culture, therefore, which leads to the idea of the *State*. In *Barbarians*,

Philistines, Populace Arnold further discusses the characteristics of the three classes of English society. They must not be too sharply differentiated. He is himself properly a Philistine, but when he has a gun or fishing-rod in his hands, he feels that he might have within him the seeds of a Barbarian, and anyone who finds himself failing in the amenities of controversy cannot but be conscious that he has found in his own bosom the eternal spirit of the populace. A few, in all three classes, have a curiosity about their best selves, a bent for the pursuit of perfection. It is genius, or at least talent. They have humanity. They get generally a rough time in their lives. They are aliens. Everything around them encourages them to keep the natural taste for bathos unimpaired. He has pointed out elsewhere how the absence of an academy tends to do this in literature. It is so, too, in religion and even more in politics. He suggests once more that to make the *State* the organ of our best self or right reason would help. In *Hebraism and Hellenism* he notes the rival contributions of Jewish and Greek thought to the enlightenment of mankind. They pursue the same aim by different courses. One contributes energy, the other intelligence. The uppermost idea with Hellenism is to see things as they really are. With Hebraism it is conduct and obedience. Hellenism is full of sweetness and light. Hebraism lays its stress on sin. Neither is in itself the law of human development, but both make august contributions to it. By the alternations of these the human spirit proceeds. *Porro Unum est Necessarium* further elaborates the same theme. No doubt we ought to praise Hebraism most. But we have already in Puritanism its fire and strength, even to excess. What we now most need is the development of our Hellenizing instincts, seeking ardently the intelligible law of things, and making a stream of fresh thought play freely about our stock notions and habits. On all sides, therefore, the more we go into the matter, the currents seem to converge, and together to bear us along towards culture. In *Our Liberal Practitioners* the doctrine here set forth is applied to some current topics. In a *Preface* of 1869 Arnold defends himself against some criticism from a religious and largely a Nonconformist angle. He does not, he thinks, undervalue Hebraism. Now, and for us, it is a time to Hellenize, and to praise knowing; for we have Hebraized too much, and have over-valued doing. But the habits and discipline received from Hebraism remain for our race an eternal possession; and, as humanity is constituted, one must never assign to them the second rank to-day without being prepared to restore them the first rank to-morrow. Let us conclude by marking this distinctly. To walk staunchly by the best light one has, to be strict and sincere with oneself, not to be of the number of those who say and do not, to be in earnest—this is the discipline by which alone man is enabled to rescue his life from thraldom to the passing moment and to his bodily senses, to ennoble it, and to make it eternal. And this discipline has been nowhere so effectively taught as in the school of Hebraism.

Arnold's definition of culture as sweetness and light attracted attention. He describes a dinner-party, at which he met Benjamin Disraeli:

'Dizzy' was in high force and it was agreeable. He said to me across the table, *à propos* of something that was mentioned, 'Sweetness and light I call that, Mr. Arnold, eh?'

And when he was given the honorary degree of D.C.L. at the Oxford Commemoration of 1870, Lord Salisbury, then Chancellor of the University, told him that he ought to have addressed him as *Vir dulcissime et lucidissime*.

Culture was not Arnold's only subject for disquisition in 1869. Late in the year he contributed two short articles to the *Academy*. One was on Étienne Pivert de Senancour, the French writer of the letters of *Obermann* and *Libres Méditations d'un Solitaire Inconnu*. In him Arnold seems to have taken an interest from the time of his visits to George Sand and to Switzerland in 1846, the year of Senancour's death at Sèvres, where his tomb bore the inscription, *Éternité, deviens mon asile*. He was reading *Obermann* in 1848. A copy of George Sand's 1840 edition was among his books. In 1849 he wrote and in 1852 published his *Stanzas in Memory of the Author of Obermann*, in which he compared Senancour's 'icy despair' at 'the hopeless tangle of our age' with Wordsworth's 'sweet calm' and Goethe's 'wide and luminous view'. In his *New Poems* of 1867 appeared *Obermann Once More*, written after another visit to Senancour's haunts in Switzerland, some twenty years later. Here Obermann is

> Thou master of my wandering youth,
> But left this many a year!

Senancour's constant pessimism about the future of the world was not quite Arnold's temper at this time. But he now gets from him a vision of an ideal order in which the desire of men is satisfied in harmony. In 1867 he had written to a friend of the extraordinary impression which Senancour's works had made on him at the age of twenty-five, but denied that he merely used Obermann as a mouthpiece for his own opinions. And in the same year he complained to his mother that some critics had calmly said of Obermann's speeches and of those of Empedocles, 'Mr. Arnold here professes his Pantheism', or 'Mr. Arnold here disowns Christianity'. In the second edition of *New Poems* (1868) he gave a short sketch of Senancour's life, noting his profound inwardness and austere sincerity. He was haunted by St. Bernard's question '*Bernarde, ad quid venisti?*', and could find no answer. We have seen that Senancour's '*Périssons en résistant*' had impressed Arnold. The *Academy* article does not add very much to the notice of 1868. Senancour felt the bare and bleak spiritual atmosphere into which he was born. He had a passion for order and harmony.

La tendance à l'ordre ne peut-elle faire une partie essentielle de nos inclinations, de notre instinct, comme la tendance à la conservation, à la reproduction?

But he became discouraged, both with religion and civil society. The time was out of joint, *Vos douleurs ont flétri mon âme*. His poetic emotion and deep feeling for nature sometimes relieved him.

The second *Academy* article of 1869 was on Charles Augustin Sainte-Beuve, a French student of literature and philosophy, with whom Arnold had been in correspondence and who had given a prose translation of the first *Obermann* poem in his *Chateaubriand et son groupe littéraire* of 1861.

And by the end of 1869 Arnold had turned from culture to begin the long series of writings on religion which were in the end to give him the reputation of a heretic. The first two articles of *St. Paul and Protestantism* appeared in the *Cornhill* for October and November. Arnold wrote to his mother that he was much touched by her willingness, as always, to receive and comprehend what was new, instead of shutting her mind against it. A third instalment on *Puritanism and the Church of England* was intended for Christmas, but was apparently deferred to February 1870. In the same month Arnold sent his mother some lines of verse from the second article which are worth quoting here because they revert to his old theme of the River of Life and did not get into his collected *Poems*.

> Below the surface-stream, shallow and light,
> Of what we *say* we feel—below the stream,
> As light, of what we *think* we feel there flows
> With noiseless current strong, obscure, and deep,
> The central stream of what we feel indeed.

By June 1870 the book was published and was doing very well. Its *Preface* had been discussed by Nonconformists at their May meetings. As the book stands in the popular edition of 1887 it has only a short *Preface*. The original one has become a separate chapter, called *Modern Dissent*, and *A Comment on Christmas*, originally contributed to the *Contemporary Review* in 1885, has been added.

The Arminius letters to the *Pall Mall Gazette* were continued in 1870, with more about the Philistines. But now Arnold killed off Arminius. The whole series was reprinted, with some other matter, in his *Friendship's Garland* of 1871. A lecture at Birmingham in the same year, on *A Persian Passion Play*, published in the *Cornhill* for December and later reprinted in the third edition (1875) of *Essays in Criticism*, led to a short correspondence with Cardinal Newman, to whom Arnold sent a copy with a grateful recognition of the interest which he had felt in the Cardinal's sermons at Oxford during his early days. In 1872 he followed this with a copy of a little book on Isaiah, called *A Bible Reading for Schools: The Great Prophecy of Israel's Restoration*. Newman, he said, was one of the four people from whom he had learnt habits, methods, and ruling ideas which were constantly with him. The others were Goethe, Wordsworth, and Sainte-Beuve. Newman was gracious in his replies. In 1872 Arnold contributed to a periodical called *Every Saturday* an article on the French theological writer, Ernest Renan.

In 1871 Arnold also began in the *Cornhill* his *Literature and Dogma*, which was to carry on the theme of *St. Paul and Protestantism*. It ran through 1872 and was published in book form by February 1873. It attracted much attention and went rapidly through three editions. In December he was writing a preface for a fourth edition. In November 1874 he was contemplating the issue of a cheaper one. But of this he wrote that, should he decide to publish it, which he was not disposed to do at present, he should very likely cut out all which he thought was not directly essential to the argument of the book.

A shortened popular edition first appeared in 1883,

with a new preface. The full title is *Literature and Dogma: An Essay towards a Better Apprehension of the Bible*. Even in this form it is a long book of twelve chapters with an Introduction and a Conclusion. For a motto Arnold prefixed the sentence by Senancour on instinct which I have already quoted.

In April 1874 Arnold was planning to answer criticisms of *Literature and Dogma* in the *Contemporary Review*. This ran on to September 1875 and was then reprinted as *God and the Bible*. Again a shortened popular edition followed in 1884, with an arrangement similar to that of its predecessor. The *Bible Reading for Schools* of 1872 was revised in 1875, with an addition of the shorter prophecies in *Isaiah*. In 1876 came five lectures and essays of minor importance, which were collected in 1877 as *Last Essays on Church and Religion*. In a Preface Arnold said that the book closed his attempts to deal directly with questions concerning religion and the Church. But, in returning to devote to literature, strictly so called, what remained to him of life and strength and leisure, he thought that he was, after all, returning to a field where important work had still to be done, though indirectly, for religion. The transformation of religion, essential for its perpetuance, could only be accomplished by carrying the qualities of flexibility, perceptiveness, and judgement, which are the best fruits of letters, to classes of the community which knew next to nothing of them, and by procuring the application of those qualities to matters where they were never applied at present.

I do not propose to attempt any continuous analysis of Arnold's long disquisitions on religion. It must be sufficient to trace the development of his ideas on their two main subjects, Miracles and the Concept of God. As far as possible I shall use his own words. I have already noted his tendency to self-repetition for purposes of emphasis. On miracles he starts, probably about 1869, with Spinoza.

To the multitude, religion seems imposing only when it is subversive of reason, confirmed by miracles, conveyed in documents materially sacred and infallible, and dooming to damnation all without its pale. But this religion of the multitude is not the religion which a true interpretation of Scripture finds in Scripture. Reason tells us that a miracle,—understanding by a miracle a breach of the laws of nature,—is impossible, and that to think it possible is to dishonour God; for the laws of nature are the laws of God, and to say that God violates the laws of nature is to say that God violates his own nature.

Spinoza's further argument he thinks perplexing to the attentive reader, who feels that Spinoza, proceeding on an hypothesis, has presented him with the assertion of a miracle, and afterwards, proceeding *a priori*, has presented him with the assertion that a miracle is impossible.

Arnold's own views first appear in *St. Paul and Protestantism*. Puritanism maintains 'that Paul's doctrines derive their sanction from his miraculous conversion, which in his own judgment gave to them their authority'. But 'for science, his conversion adds to his doctrines no force at all which they do not already possess in themselves'. Later he says, 'For popular theology the force of Christ's resurrection is that it is a miracle which guarantees the promised future miracle of our own resurrection. It is a common remark, even with able and candid Biblical critics, that Christ's resurrection, in this sense of a physical miracle, is the central object of Paul's thoughts and the foundation of all his theology.' He thinks that this rests on a perversion of the *Epistle to the Romans*. He admits that in Paul's earlier theology 'the physical and miraculous aspect of the resurrection, both Christ's and the believer's, is primary and predominant', and that he may have accepted it, 'as well as in his own spiritual and mystical sense', to the end of his life. But in the *Epistle* 'the resurrection Paul was striving after was a resurrection *now* and a resurrection to *righteousness*'. He adds, however, later, 'That Paul accepted the physical miracle of Christ's resurrection and ascension as a part of the signs and wonders which accompanied Christianity there can be no doubt'.

In *Literature and Dogma* he is discussing *Aberglaube* or 'extra-belief' on things not certain. Man pays for it, when he discovers its uncertainty, and the basis of conduct has gone. 'This danger attends the reliance on prediction and miracle as evidences of Christianity.' Men have said and thought that the order of physical nature is not fate, nor a mere material constitution of things, but the subject of a free omnipotent Master. As regards miracles the reliance on this breaks down. 'The substitution of some other proof of Christianity for this accustomed proof is now to be desired most by those who most think Christianity of importance.' But his main discussion of 'the proof from miracles' comes later in the book. 'That miracles, when fully believed, are felt by men in general to be a source of authority, it is absurd to deny. But the belief is losing its strength. It is what we call the *Time-Spirit* which is sapping the proof from miracles—it is the Zeit-Geist itself. Whether we attack them, or whether we defend them, does not much matter. The human race, as its experience widens, is turning away from them. And for this reason: *it sees, as its experience increases, how they arise.*' The objections will make their force felt, 'and the sanction of Christianity, if Christianity is not to be lost along with its miracles, must be found elsewhere'. He doubts whether Jesus relied on miracles. But, as Christianity spread, it 'developed more and more its side of miracle and legend'.

In 1874 Arnold wrote to a sister who had charged him with treating with lightness what was matter of life and death to so many people:

There is a levity, which is altogether evil; but to treat miracles and the common anthropomorphic ideas of God as what one may lose and yet keep one's hope, courage and joy, as what

are not really matters of life and death in the keeping or
losing of them, this is desirable and necessary, if one holds, as I
do, that the common anthropomorphic ideas of God and the
reliance on miracles must and will inevitably pass away.

Perhaps Arnold's instinct for a phrase did sometimes lead
him into levity in writing of serious subjects.

In the chapter on *The God of Miracles* in *God and the
Bible*, he justifies himself for 'the brevity and moderation'
with which he treated the subject in *Literature and Dogma*.
He thinks the thesis that miracles cannot be relied upon
'though true, is merely negative, and therefore of secondary importance', and that 'the important question is,
what becomes of religion—so precious, as we believe, to
the human race—if miracles cannot be relied on'. There
is no complete induction against them, though there is an
incomplete induction, enough to satisfy the mind, that
the evidence for them is untrustworthy. We are dealing
with fairy-tales. We must look for new grounds, on
which to build religion more firmly. In a *Conclusion* he
adds that his opponents say, 'everything turns upon the
question whether miracles do or did really happen; and
you abstain from all attempt to prove their impossibility,
you simply assume that they never happen'. He admits
it, and stresses it. 'That miracles *cannot* happen we do not
attempt to prove; the demonstration is too ambitious.
That they *do not* happen—that what are called miracles
are not what the believers in them fancy, but have a
natural history of which we can follow the course—the
slow action of experience, we say, more and more shows;
and shows, too, that there is no exception to be made in
favour of the Bible-miracles.'

In a Preface of 1883 to the popular edition of *Literature
and Dogma*, he says, 'It has become even yet more mani-
fest that by the sanction of miracles Christianity can no
longer stand; it can stand only by its natural truth'. The
real concern of his book, however, is not with miracles,
but with that natural truth. And so, 'miracles have to go

the same way as clericalism and tradition: and the important thing is, not that the world should be acute enough to see this, but that a great and progressive part of the world should be capable of seeing this and of yet holding fast to Christianity'. The object of *Literature and Dogma* is 'to assist those called to such an endeavour'. He does not wish it to be regarded as an attack on miracles and the supernatural. It admits, indeed, that the belief in them has given way and cannot be restored, it recommends entire lucidity of mind on this subject, it points out certain characters of weakness in the sanction drawn from miracles, even while the belief in them lasted. Its real concern, however, is not with miracles, but with the natural truth of Christianity. And his final word in the *Preface* is, 'Our popular religion at present conceives the birth, ministry and death of Christ, as altogether steeped in prodigy, brimful of miracle;—*and miracles do not happen*'. In his *Comment on Christmas* of 1885 he complained of 'an angry and unreasonable expostulation', in which he was reproached for saying that more and more of us are becoming convinced of this, and for adding, 'Nevertheless what is really best and most valuable in the Bible is independent of miracles, and for the sake of this, I constantly read the Bible myself, and I advise others to read it also'.

And now for Arnold's definition of God. In *St. Paul and Protestantism* he says, 'The licence of affirmation about God and his proceedings, in which the religious world indulge, is more and more met by the demand for verification'. Calvinism tells us, 'It is agreed between God and the Mediator Jesus Christ, the Son of God, surety for the redeemed, as parties-contractors, that the sins of the redeemed should be imputed to innocent Christ, and he both condemned and put to death for them, upon this very condition, that whosoever heartily consents unto the covenant of conciliation offered through Christ, shall, by the imputation of his obedience unto them, be justified and holden righteous before God'. But, when Calvinism tells us this, 'is it not talking about God just as if he were a man in the next street, whose proceedings Calvinism intimately knew and could give account of, could verify that account at any moment and enable us to verify it also'? No one will deny that the scientific sense in us, the sense which seeks exact knowledge, calls for that verification, although many will deplore it. It is not that the scientific sense in us denies the rights of the poetic sense, which employs a figured and imaginative language. But the language we have just been quoting is not figurative and poetic language, it is scholastic and scientific language. Assertions in scientific language must stand the tests of scientific examination. Neither is it that the scientific sense in us refuses to admit willingly and reverently the name of God as a point in which the religious and the scientific sense may meet, as the least inadequate name for that universal order which the intellect feels after as a law and the heart feels after as a benefit. We too, might the men of science say to the men of religion—we too would gladly say *God*, if only, the moment one says *God*, you would not pester one with your pretensions of knowing all about him. 'That *stream of tendency by which all things seek to fulfil the law of their being*, and which, inasmuch as our idea of real welfare resolves itself into this fulfilment of the law of one's being, man rightly deems the fountain of all goodness, and calls by the worthiest and most solemn name he can, which is God, science also might willingly own for the fountain of all goodness, and call God. But however much more than this the heart may with propriety put into its language respecting God, this is as much as science can with strictness put there.' Later in the book he notes that Calvinists allow more than some of their theological opponents 'for the great fact of the *not ourselves* in what we do and are', and still later notes St. Paul's 'consciousness of that power, *not ourselves*, in which we live and move

and have our being'. He thinks 'the notion of God as a
magnificent and non-natural man, appeased by a sacrifice, and remitting in consideration of it his wrath against
those who had offended him—this notion of God, which
science repels, was equally repelled by the profound
religious sense of Paul'.

In *Literature and Dogma* he notes an 'incurable ambi-
guity' in the use of the term *God*. Philologically the
Aryan word God means 'shining' or 'brilliant'. It was
long thought to mean 'good'. Luther defined it as 'the
best that man knows or can know'. This is the word's
real sense, although it does not give anything very precise.
Modern philology does not quite bear him out here,
preferring to relate the word to one or other of two
Aryan roots, one meaning 'to invoke', the other 'to pour,
to offer sacrifice'. But he goes on to note a scientific
sense held by theologians, in which 'God is an infinite
and eternal substance, and at the same time a person,
the great first cause, the moral and intelligent governor
of the universe', having 'Jesus Christ consubstantial with
him', and the Holy Ghost 'a person proceeding from the
other two'. Later, he says that the Old Testament is full
of the word and thought of righteousness. Those who
spoke of it could not fail to be struck by 'the very great
part of righteousness which belongs, we may say, to *not
ourselves*'. And this *not ourselves* becomes practically his
definition of 'God'. It inspired Israel with awe, as the
source from which we get the sense for righteousness and
the help to do right. This conception led to the Hebrew
name *The Eternal*, which we wrongly convey by *Jehovah*
or *Lord*. They simply meant the 'not ourselves' as a
power which makes for righteousness. It is true that the
'not ourselves' of which we are thankfully conscious we
inevitably speak of and to as a man, for 'man never
knows how anthropomorphic he is', and as time went
on imagination and reason kept working upon this
substructure, and built from it a magnificent and

non-natural man. Israel, then, 'knew from thankful experience the *not ourselves*, which makes for righteousness, and knew how little we know about God besides'. He has been blamed for saying that, for science, God is simply, 'the stream of tendency by which all things seek to fulfil the law of their being'. It is inadequate, but 'in however humble a degree and with however narrow a reach a scientific definition'. No doubt 'a personal First Cause, the moral and intelligent Governor of the universe' has also the character of a scientific definition. But it 'goes far beyond what is admittedly certain and verifiable, which is what we mean by scientific'. On the other hand 'that all things seem to us to have what we call a law of their being, and to tend to fulfil it, is certain and admitted, though whether we call it *God* or not, is a matter of choice'. But at least we get a starting-ground in 'an enduring power, not ourselves, which makes for righteousness'. Jesus himself by no means gave a new, more precise, definition of God than Israel had done, but took up the term to stand for *The Eternal* that loveth righteousness. But, though this grand conception of God meets the need of three-fourths of our being, there is one-fourth which it does not, that which is concerned with art and science, or in other words, with beauty and exact knowledge. 'For the total man, therefore, the truer conception of God is as the Eternal Power, not ourselves, by which all things fulfil the law of their being; by which, therefore, we fulfil the law of our being so far as our being is aesthetic and intellective, as well as so far as it is moral.'

Finally, we have *God and the Bible*. Here Arnold says,

'Many excellent people are crying out everyday that all is lost in religion unless we can affirm that God is a person who thinks and loves. We say, that unless we can verify this, it is impossible to build religion successfully upon it; and it cannot be verified. Even if it could be shown that there is a low degree of probability for it, we say that it is a grave and fatal error to imagine that religion can be built on what has a low degree of probability. However, we do not think it can be said that there is even a low degree of probability for the assertion that God is a person who thinks and loves, properly and naturally though we may make him such in the language of feeling; the assertion deals with what is so utterly beyond us. But we maintain, that, starting from what may be verified about God,—that he is the Eternal which makes for righteousness,—and reading the Bible with this idea to govern us, we have here the elements for a religion more serious, potent, awe-inspiring, and profound, than any which the world has yet seen. True, it will not be just the same religion which prevails now; but who supposes that the religion now current can go on always, or ought to go on? Nay, and even of that much-decried idea of God as *the stream of tendency by which all things seek to fulfil the law of their being*, it may be said with confidence that it has in it the elements of a religion new, indeed, but in the highest hopeful, solemn, and profound.

And later in the book, 'We are accused of introducing in the *not ourselves* a refined metaphysical conception. It is so far from this that it is one of the first pieces of man's experience, and dates from the most primitive time. It is whatever appears to man as outside himself, not in his own power, and affecting him whether he will or no.' And he asks, 'Who first, amid the loose solicitations of sense, obeyed (for create it he did not) the mighty *not ourselves* which makes for moral order, the stream of tendency which was here carrying him, and our embryo race along with him, towards the fulfilment of the true law of their being?—became aware of it and obeyed it?'

I am a little puzzled by Arnold's 'not ourselves'. As I have already said, he used as a motto for *Literature and Dogma* a saying of Senancour, which I have already given, and will give again here.

La tendance à l'ordre ne peut-elle faire une partie essentielle de nos inclinations, de notre instinct, comme la tendance à la conservation, à la reproduction?

I should have rather expected him to hold that the human tendency to righteousness came from no outside source, but was part of our 'instinct'. Wyndham Slade recorded in a slip found in his copy of *God and the Bible*, that Arnold's wife once said, 'Matt is a good Christian at bottom'. It is no doubt true that he accepted most of the moral doctrine of Christianity, apart from its *Aberglaube.*

VII

THE LAST YEARS

ARNOLD did not find it quite so easy as he had anticipated, when he wrote a preface for his last religious *Essays*, to devote himself in future to 'literature more strictly so called'. He refused a request to stand again for the Professorship of Poetry at Oxford, on the ground that the religious question would certainly be raised, and that this would be bad for the University and intolerable for himself. But he had acquired the reputation of a competent and even amusing lecturer, and found it difficult —perhaps could not well afford—to reject applications for his services in that capacity. However that may be, his activities during the next two or three years continued to cover a wide range of topics. I shall not go into great detail about the subject-matter of most of them.

During the first half of 1877 he wrote articles on Edmond Scherer, as *A French Critic on Milton*, on Lucius Cary, Lord Falkland, on one Wiese's *German Letters on English Education*, and on George Sand. Of her he now told his wife, 'She is beginning to weigh upon me greatly, though she also interests me very much; the old feeling of liking for her and of refreshment from her, in spite of all her faults, comes back'. In December he reviewed Stopford Brooke's *A Guide to English Literature*. He contemplated also a collection of old sermons, to be called *Broad Church in the Seventeenth Century*, although I do not know whether it ever appeared.

In January 1878 he wrote again on Scherer, this time as *A French Critic on Goethe*, and also contributed a preface to an edition of the *Six Chief Lives* from Samuel Johnson's *Lives of the Poets*. But his chief work during this year was once more in social philosophy. His *Equality* was a lecture at the Royal Institution. It was an argument against unlimited freedom in the bequest of landed property. He cites the maxim of Menander, 'Choose equality and flee greed', which he interprets as wanting 'the bigger share'. English statesmen, including both Gladstone and Disraeli, are against equality, although France aims at it in social matters, and George Sand thought the pre-eminence of France in civilization owing to it. English families with great estates preserve inequality by entail and settlement under the right to freedom of bequest. French law forbids entail. A man must divide all but a quarter of his property among his children. Similar restrictions prevail in some other European countries, and even in Australia. He recites his own classification of English social classes as Barbarians, Philistines, and Populace, but qualifies it by noting the existence, in the professions, services, literature, politics, and even business, of a large class, who have a high standard of civilization, but are not of the nobility. This is certainly, I think, an improvement on his earlier doctrine. He does not claim equality as a 'natural right', does not in fact believe in 'natural rights', either for peasants or workmen, or for kings and nobles. Property is created and maintained by law. Some inequality is inevitable, but it should not be unlimited or enormous. France has come to fearful troubles, but not through social equality. Nations advance towards full humanity on different lines, Hellenes on 'the power of intellect and science, the power of beauty, the power of social life and manners', Hebrews on 'the power of conduct'. The French, too, have 'the power of social intercourse and manners', which leads to equality. The French peasants are ignorant, but have intelligence, excellent manners, delicate perceptions, tact, a certain refinement. But in England a cultivated person, talking to one of the lower or even middle class, feels a wall of partition between them. But the power of social life and manners is only

one element in civilization. The French have not a
similar sense, either for the power of conduct or for the
power of beauty. Hence their dangers and troubles. As
for ourselves, we have a sense for the power of conduct.
We have a rich, refined, splendid, but materialized
aristocracy, and a class of gentlemen, not of the nobility,
but well-bred, cultivated, and refined. Our middle class
has a gay and rowdy portion, whose standard of life may
be judged by the modern English theatre, perhaps the
most contemptible in Europe. But its real strength is in
its serious portion. To a Frenchman this appears to want
elasticity, to be 'petrified in a narrow Protestantism and
in a perpetual reading of the Bible'. Perhaps a little more
Biblism would do the French no harm. But it is true, as
I have said before and may say again, that in the seventeenth century the middle class 'entered the prison of
Puritanism, and had the key turned upon its spirit there
for two hundred years'. And he adds,

Those who offer us the Puritan type of life offer us a religion
not true, the claims of intellect and knowledge not satisfied, the
claim of beauty not satisfied, the claim of manners not satisfied.
In its strong sense for conduct that life touches truth, but its
other imperfections hinder it from employing even that sense
aright.

The type mastered the whole nation for a time. Then it
retired into our middle class and fortified itself there.
If we are to continue to live we must outgrow it. We
have a splendid aristocratic class, with conspicuous
examples of individuals raised by happy gifts of nature
far above their fellows and their circumstances. But on
the whole it is materialized, and even for politics has not
sufficient acquaintance with the ideas which in the end
survey mankind. Nor can a materialized class have any
serious and fruitful sense for the power of beauty. For
the power of manners it has a strong one. The large class
of gentlemen, not of the landed class or of the nobility,
to whom he has referred, are more seriously alive to

the powers of intellect, knowledge, and beauty. But even
they tend to become materialized. They are deficient in
openness and flexibility of mind, in free play of ideas, in
faith and ardour. They produce singularly little effect
on the middle class. These are thrown back on themselves, on a defective type of religion, a narrow range of
intellect and knowledge. The lower classes see both of
the others out of their reach. They are thrown back on
their beer, their gin, and their fun. He thinks the time
has come for some better ideal of life in the middle class.
'Certainly equality will never by itself give us a perfect
civilisation. But, with such inequality as ours, a perfect
civilisation is impossible.' He thinks that a law of
bequest fixing the maximum which any one individual
may take by inheritance, but in other respects leaving the
testator free, would be preferable to the actual French
method.

Later in 1878 he wrote two articles for the *Fortnightly*.
One, *Porro Unum est Necessarium*, was on the need to provide good public schools for the middle classes. In the
other, *Irish Catholicism and British Liberalism*, he touched
on a theme which was to occupy him much to the end of
his life, that of the political relations between England
and Ireland. Charles Stewart Parnell had already
started on his tactics of obstructing all business in the
House of Commons, as a step towards his goal of Irish
independence. The immediate issue was on his demand
for an Act to enable tenants of the disestablished Irish
Church to buy their holdings. Arnold saw that behind
this lay the prejudice of the English middle class against
Irish Catholicism. He agreed that all the mischiefs of
Catholicism were rampant in Ireland, but thought
that a remedy might lie in giving the Irish public schools
and a national University, with Catholic professors,
nominated, not by the bishops, but by a minister of
state.

In 1879 Arnold issued a volume of *Mixed Essays*. Here

he reprinted the *Preface* to his Educational Report of
1861, with the title of *Democracy*, and also his *Equality* of
1878, together with four other articles of 1877 and three
of 1878. In a Preface he stressed once more, as the conditions of civilization, the instinct of expansion, including
both liberty and equality, and the powers of conduct,
intellect, and knowledge, beauty and social life and
manners. He also gave two lectures. One, to the
Ipswich Working-men's College, was once more on the
need for equality, on the want of 'openness and flexibility
of mind' in the middle class, and on a possible remedy
through the provision of public secondary schools. He
called it *Ecce, Convertimur ad Gentes*. The other was to the
Eton Literary Society. This was again on the need for
'flexibility', the εὐτραπελία of the Greeks. The word first
appeared in the Funeral Oration put by Thucydides into the mouth of Pericles. Flexibility implies lucidity of
thought, clearness and propriety of language, freedom
from prejudice and stiffness, openness of mind, amiability
of manners, but not, as we English are apt to think, a
relaxation of moral fibre. St. Paul used the word εὐτραπελία in a depreciatory sense for jesting, one of the things
which are 'not convenient'. He repeats his list of the
powers which make for civilization, but adds that of these
conduct is 'three-fourths of life'. The later Athenians
forgot this. On the other hand medievalism took no
account of flexibility. He draws a moral. Man has to
make progress along diverse lines, in obedience to a
diversity of aspirations and powers, the sum of which is
truly his nature; and he fails and falls short until he
learns to advance upon them all, and to advance upon
them harmoniously. It was a gracious utterance to a
congenial audience.

In 1879 Arnold did also find time for some work on
literature, 'more strictly so called'. He compiled a selection from the poems of Wordsworth, as one of a series of
volumes known as the Golden Treasury, and added an

elaborate critical preface. Arnold gave Wordsworth a
very high place among English poets. His early vogue at
Cambridge, due largely to the influence of Coleridge,
waned rather after the appearance of Tennyson, and
he has not yet obtained his full deserts. Abroad, Shakespeare and Milton are recognized, but not yet Wordsworth. Arnold will not compare him with Chaucer, who
belongs to an earlier age, but, after going through the roll
of poetic names from Spenser to Keats, he thinks that
Wordsworth's will finally stand above them all. And if
we take into account the chief poetic names of the Continent, with the exception of Goethe, it seems to him that
Wordsworth has left a body of poetical work which will
wear better than that of any one of them. His reputation
has suffered from the intermixture of his best poems with
inferior ones. Arnold does not think his *Excursion* and
Prelude so good as many of his shorter pieces. But he
needs to be relieved of baggage. His own classification of
his poems, according to a scheme of mental physiology,
as of the fancy, of the imagination, of sentiment and
reflection, and so on, is ingenious, but far-fetched and
unsatisfactory. Here I heartily agree with Arnold. A
critical edition of the poems, in the order of their publication, is much to be desired. But what strikes him most,
and establishes in his opinion Wordsworth's superiority,
is the 'great and ample body of powerful work which
remains to him, after the inferior work has been cleared
away. The object of his selection is to isolate this.
Wordsworth's superiority rests on the powerful use, in his
best pieces, of ideas 'on man, on nature, and on human
life'. Arnold recalls his own definition of poetry as 'a
criticism of life'. Wordsworth's superiority over other
English poets lies in this, that he deals with more of *life*
than they do; he deals with it, as a whole, more power-
fully. Wordsworth's formal philosophy he dismisses
lightly. 'The poetry is great, because of the extraordinary
power with which Wordsworth feels the joy offered to us

in nature, the joy offered to us in the simple primary
affections and duties; and because of the extraordinary
power with which, in case after case, he shows us this joy,
and renders it so as to make us share it.' Arnold is here
on the verge of recognizing the importance of the con-
veyance of emotion in poetry, although he does not use
the phrase. He repeats that some of the poems, which
reverent Wordsworthians praise, are failures. To give
what he wishes successfully is not always within his command. It is within no poet's command; here is the part
of the muse, the inspiration, the God, the 'not ourselves'.
Wordsworth's poetry, at its best, is as inevitable as nature
itself. He has no style, but he has something which is an
equivalent for it. 'Nature herself seems to take the pen
out of his hand, and to write for him with her own bare,
sheer, penetrating power.'

The book was successful financially. By 1881 7,000
copies had been sold. To 1879 also belongs a criticism of
modern drama, called *The French Play in London*. Arnold
did not think Sarah Bernhardt an equal to the Rachel of
his youth.

Early in 1880 he wrote an article on *Copyright* in
England and America, which was naturally a subject of
interest to him as a bookman. Later a general election
brought the Liberal party into power, with Gladstone as
Prime Minister, and Forster as Chief Secretary for Ireland. Arnold commented on the prospect in *The Future of
Liberalism*. He was not optimistic. He thought himself a
Liberal of the future, rather than of the present. He sur-
veyed the attitudes of the two political parties to what he
had so often described as the powers of civilization, and
concluded that when the Liberals had learnt to give full
recognition to all these, their governments would be safe.
Until then the Tories would be tried from time to time,
and found wanting.

Towards the end of the year he was again able to turn
his attention to literature, 'strictly so called'. Thomas

Humphry Ward, whose wife Mary was a daughter of
Arnold's brother Thomas, was engaged upon an exten-
sive anthology, entitled *The English Poets*, and to this
Arnold agreed to contribute a general Introduction on
The Study of Poetry, and shorter individual notices of
Thomas Gray and John Keats. It was congenial work to
him, and *The Study of Poetry*, in particular, contains some
of his best critical writing. I can only give a brief summary. He begins with a reference to an earlier statement
of his own, in which he had noted the waning of religion,
and the need for poetry to replace it. 'The strongest part
of our religion to-day is its unconscious poetry.' And he
still thinks that 'more and more mankind will discover
that we have to turn to poetry to interpret life for us, to
console us, to sustain us'. He notes Wordsworth's defini-
tions of poetry as 'the impassioned expression which is in
the countenance of all science', and 'the breath and finer
spirit of all knowledge'. And he adds his own, with which
we are already familiar, that poetry is a 'criticism of life',
under the conditions fixed by the laws of poetic truth and
poetic beauty. We must beware of the historic estimate
and the personal estimate, both of which are fallacious.
Certain passages from the great masters are an infallible
touchstone. He gives examples. He lays stress on Aristotle's statement that the superiority of poetry over
history consists in its possessing a higher truth and a
higher seriousness. These are generalities, which he
wants every student of poetry to apply for himself. He
notes the predominance of French poetry in the twelfth
and thirteenth centuries, and the emergence of Chaucer
in the fourteenth, but will not here discuss the Eliza-
bethans and Milton. I do not quite know why. In the
age of Dryden and Pope verse becomes subordinate to
prose. He deals at some length with Burns, who, in spite
of the hideousness, squalor, and bestiality, has largeness,
freedom, archness and wit, and infinite pathos. I do not
know why he lays so much stress on Burns. In a letter to

his sister he describes him more briefly, as 'a beast, with splendid gleams'. He will not, in this study, approach the 'burning ground' of other contemporary poetry, such as that of Byron, Shelley, and Wordsworth.

With Arnold's comments on Gray and Keats I must deal more summarily. Gray 'never spoke out'. That is his whole history, as man and poet. Samuel Johnson's *Life* of him was unsympathetic, and other contemporaries valued him more highly. His *Elegy written in a Country Churchyard* is not his best work. His production was scanty. He had a wide range of learning, and was a great antiquarian. He has been described as the first discoverer of the beauties of nature in England. He knew the Greek classics. He wrote better on Shakespeare than most critics of his time. He had a sense of humour. But he was melancholy, and with all his great qualities 'he never spoke out'. He was doomed to sterility, a poet in an age of prose. Keats was sensuous, and lacking in self-control. By his promise, if not his performance, he was one of the greatest of English poets. He could show admirable wisdom and temper upon occasion, and criticize his own work with strength and clearness. He agreed that his *Endymion* was 'slipshod'. He said that he had no trust whatever in poetry. But he rather undervalued himself. His bitterness and defiance were subdued and corrected when he wrote his beautiful preface to *Endymion*. He had clear-sightedness and lucidity. 'The best sort of poetry', he said, 'is all I care for, all I live for.' He was cold to love and women. His 'yearning passion for the Beautiful' was an intellectual and spiritual, not a sensuous or senti-mental one. But he claimed to have 'loved the principle of beauty in all things', and perceived the necessary relation of beauty with truth, and of both with joy. Through this insight he ranks in natural magic with Shakespeare, although he has not Shakespeare's faculty of moral interpretation.

In 1880 appeared a volume of *Passages from the Prose*

Writings of Matthew Arnold. In 1881 came a selection from Byron on the same lines as that from Wordsworth. Arnold did not think that one from Scott or Shelley would be of equal value. He agrees with Shelley in thinking Byron a greater poetical power than himself. Shelley has more loveliness and charm, but also more unsubstantiality. But, like Wordsworth, Byron gains by selection. His power is not in the artistic creation of poetic wholes, but in the vivid conception of single incidents or situations. His vogue has passed, but we can bring his best and strongest work together. Much of his production is slovenly and tuneless, and as a man he was vulgar and affected. But that is not the whole truth. Goethe thought him the greatest talent of our century, but that the moment he began to reflect he was a child. With all but the supreme masters whose poetry is a criticism of life we have to strike a balance. Arnold agrees with Swinburne that the power of Byron's personality lies in his excellence of sincerity and strength. He was revolted by the cant of middle-class Philistinism, but even more by the cant of his own class, deferring to this Philistinism, and profiting by it, while they disbelieved in it. In life he was a poser, but when at work he showed his 'true and puissant personality, with its direct strokes, its ever-welling force, its satire, its energy, and its agony'. He was not an artist, but when he warmed to his work, and was inspired, Nature herself seemed to take the pen from him. Wordsworth and Byron, concludes Arnold, stand 'first and pre-eminent, a glorious pair', among the English poets of their century. Keats had probably a more consummate poetic gift than either of them, but he died immature. Arnold will not equal with his 'glorious pair', either Coleridge, 'poet and philosopher wrecked in a mist of opium', or Shelley 'beautiful and ineffectual angel, beating in the void his luminous wings in vain'. I doubt whether, so far as Byron is concerned, posterity has confirmed, or will confirm, Arnold's verdict.

And now, still in 1881, Arnold became, once more, immersed in Irish politics. Gladstone had introduced a Coercion Bill, and another for fixing fair rents in Ireland. Arnold wrote two articles, one on *The Incompatibles,* the other on *An Unregarded Irish Grievance.* He emphasizes the wisdom of Burke, to an edition of whose *Letters, Speeches and Tracts on Irish Affairs* he had just written a preface. He does not think that the standard of Irish civilization is lower than that of England, on which is the curse of hardness. Goethe called the English 'pedants'. Burke insisted that our action in Ireland must be healing. He doubts whether Gladstone's measures will prove to be that. Both countries are deficient in the 'powers' of civilization, on which he again dwells at some length. In particular, if the Irish would make up their minds to have a better system of education, they would also be teaching England and the English middle class how to live.

In 1882 Arnold gave a Rede Lecture at Cambridge on *Literature and Science,* and another at University College, Liverpool, on *The Methods of Science.* He also wrote minor articles on *An Eton Boy,* and on *A French Worthy,* one Rapet, a School Inspector, and a criticism of *The Silver King,* under the signature of 'An Old Play-Goer'. More interesting than these is *A Word about America,* which shows the direction in which his mind was then beginning to turn. He also published a volume of *Irish Essays and Others,* with a Preface, in which he had a little more to say about the Irish Land Act. Besides his two latest essays on Ireland, he here included his *Speech at Eton* and *French Play in London* of 1879, his *Future of Liberalism* and *Copyright* of 1880, and the Prefaces to his volumes of Poems, compiled as far back as 1853 and 1854. In 1883 came some more dramatic criticism, an address to the Wordsworth Society at Westminster, printed in *Macmillan's,* and a third little book on *Isaiah,* completing his version of the entire work. But he was now largely occupied with preparations for an intended visit to America, in the course of which he purposed to give some lectures. Presumably he had obtained a long vacation from the Education Office for this purpose, in consideration of his consent to defer his retirement from his Inspectorship to 1886. By October he had written a discourse on *Numbers: or The Majority and the Remnant*, and fitted a new introduction to his Rede Lecture on *Literature and Science*. A third discourse was to be on Emerson, who he thought had been of more use to him than Carlyle, but this he had to leave for compilation in America itself. He was hopeful, having been told that all the railway porters and guards in America had read his books.

In October he sailed, working at Emerson on the ship, and by the end of the month was at New York. With him went his wife and his daughter Lucy. He lectured in a large number of towns in various parts of the States, and towards the end of his trip in Canada. Emerson was dead, but Arnold met members of his family at Concord. At first he was troubled by the difficulty of making himself audible to audiences much larger than he had been accustomed to in England. General Grant said of his first lecture, 'Well, wife, we have paid to see the British lion, we cannot hear him roar, so we had better go home'. Arnold consulted an expert, and so improved his delivery. He was amused with his special travelling tickets, which had '*Matthew Arnold troupe*' printed on them, with an invitation from the showman, Phineas Barnum, 'You, Mr. Arnold, are a celebrity, I am a notoriety; we ought to be acquainted', and with a description of himself in a Chicago newspaper—'He has harsh features, supercilious manners, parts his hair down the middle, wears a single eye-glass and ill-fitting clothes.' He reckoned that his profits would amount to about £1,000. He made many new friends. His daughter Lucy spent much time with some of them in New York, and there she became engaged to one Frederick W. Whitridge.

By November Arnold was longing to be home again, but he did not actually return until March 1884. He then sent his *Numbers* to the *Nineteenth Century*, and in October repeated his *Literature and Science* lecture at Dundee. His other literary contributions during this year were very slight. Probably he found arrears of work waiting for him at the Education Office.

In 1885 he published *Numbers, Literature and Science,* and *Emerson,* in volume form, as *Discourses in America.* During the year before his death he told George Russell that this was the book by which, of all his prose-writings, he should most wish to be remembered. Perhaps a sanguine man always tends to think his latest writings his best, but certainly *Numbers* is a fine essay. It is again on civilization, but from a new angle. Arnold is struck by the 'numbers' in America. Not that numbers anywhere are likely to be all good, or even to have the majority good. He quotes the New Testament, 'Many are called, few chosen'. And so, too, says Plato of Athens, 'There is but a very small remnant of honest followers of wisdom'. Perhaps we should have thought better of Athens, but in the end Plato proved right, and she collapsed. And so too again, Isaiah of the Hebrews, 'Though thy people Israel be as the sand of the sea, only a remnant of them shall return'. He promised better things from the coming of a Prince of the House of David, but his prophecy was not fulfilled. Both in Athens and Judah the remnant was too small to save the State. In modern states, where the scale of things is so large, it might be otherwise. But what do we mean by saving the State? Plato and the prophets know. It is to be done by loving righteousness and making one's study in the law of the Eternal.

Whatsoever things are true, whatsoever things are elevated, whatsoever things are just, whatsoever things are pure, whatsoever things are amiable, whatsoever things are of good report; if there be any virtue, and if there be any praise; have these in your mind, let your thoughts run upon these.

Politicians take little account of this. He stresses amiability. A want of this, rather than of justice, has been the
main cause of trouble between England and Ireland. In
France, where the Germanic element was not strong
enough to bring about the Reformation, it has been
lubricity. Hardness and insolence come in its train. He
turns to the United States, with its population of over
fifty millions. Here the danger is that, in a great democracy, the unsound majority will care little for the things
that are 'elevated'. Such a failure must impair with
inexorable fatality the life of a nation. He will turn to the
more comfortable doctrine of the 'remnant'. Among
fifty millions, what a remnant that of America may be!
And, as in England, the population is mainly sprung from
the Germanic stock, which he thinks, as his father thought,
the best parentage which a modern nation can have. And
America, even more than England, has had the Puritan
discipline. That has its faults, but the more he reads
history, and the more he sees of mankind, the more he
recognizes its value. 'Even supposing, therefore, that by
the necessity of things your majority must in the present
stage of the world probably be unsound, what a remnant,
I say—what an incomparable, all-transforming remnant,
—you may fairly hope with your numbers, if things go
happily, to have!'

In *Emerson*, Arnold's approach is more personal. In a
beautiful opening, he recalls the voices of his Oxford days
which haunt his memory still, the voices of Newman,
Carlyle, Goethe, and with them that of Emerson. His
poetry is not of much account. It is interesting, it makes
one think. But he is not one of the born poets. His best
passages come with a slight shock of surprise, so unusual
they are. He is not even one of the great men of letters.
He is a philosopher, although again not a great philosophical writer. But he is the friend and aider of those
who would live in the spirit. His emphasis is all on
character and self-reliance. 'Trust thyself! every heart

vibrates to that iron string', 'Life must be lived on a higher plane'. 'The unremitting retention of simple and high sentiments in obscure duties—that is the maxim for us.' The insight and truth of his judgement on the weaknesses of American life are admirable. Above all is his hopeful, serene, beautiful temper. His is the most important work done during the present century in prose, as Wordsworth's is in poetry. He has lessons both for England and for America. 'To us he shows for guidance his lucid freedom, his cheerfulness and hope; to you his dignity, delicacy, serenity, elevation.' Perhaps the circumstances in which Arnold spoke justified a little exaggeration.

In 1885 Arnold seems to have written nothing except *A Comment for Christmas*, which I have already noted as added to a late edition of *St. Paul and Protestantism*, and an account of Sainte-Beuve, which appeared in the *Encyclopaedia Britannica* during 1886. A fresh suggestion in October that he should be invited to accept a second term of the Oxford Professorship led to nothing. And now Irish politics once more took a grip upon him. By the end of 1885 Gladstone's attempts to pacify Ireland with the help of Church Disestablishment and Land Acts had failed. A General Election was due in December. Arnold thought that the Liberals would be strong in the new Parliament, but that they were unripe for power. He hoped that they would not unite with either the Tories or the Radicals. But in December he had a shock. Gladstone announced his conversion to Home Rule. 'What a move is this of Gladstone's in the Irish matter! and what apprehensions it gives me!' The election left the Liberals and Tories nearly equal in numbers, with the result that the Irish members held the balance of voting power. Lord Salisbury resigned the Premiership. Gladstone succeeded him and at once introduced his Home Rule Bill. It proposed to place the whole of Ireland under a Parliament at Dublin. This would have been a disaster for the Ulstermen of the north, who were mostly of Anglo-Saxon descent, and strongly Protestant. The English Liberal party was split. The secession of a group of members, who became Liberal Unionists, led to a defeat of the Bill, and another General Election in July 1886 brought Lord Salisbury once more into office. Arnold followed the controversy closely, and wrote many articles upon it. His first was in the *Nineteenth Century* for May 1886 on *The Nadir of Liberalism*. It was followed in the same month by a letter to *The Times* on *The Political Crisis*. In a private letter of June he drew an important distinction between giving the Irish legislative control over their own local affairs, and giving them a single legislative body to exercise such control. This would, of course, be fatal for Ulster. He thought it tragic that at this critical moment William Forster, whom he trusted, died. He was then in America. In July he again noted that there was no need, while effecting a reform, to merge Ulster in Southern Ireland. Here he is prophetic of what later became, more or less, the ultimate solution of the Irish problem. In August he wrote another letter to *The Times*, called *After the Elections*. He was amused by the heading to a summary of it in an American paper, 'Mr. M. A. favourable to Home Rule'. He returned from another short visit to America in September 1886, and in 1887 contributed three further articles on Ireland to the *Nineteenth Century*, in January, *The Zenith of Conservatism*; in May, *Up to Easter*; in September, *From Easter to August*. Here he further pressed his idea of establishing two governments in Ireland. He refused in 1887 to give any lecture or public address, but wrote some articles of minor importance on the American *General Grant*, on *A Friend of God*, one Tauler, on *Amiel*, and on *Count Leo Tolstoi*.

In 1888 he wrote an article on *Disestablishment in Wales*, and gave a lecture at Hull on *Civilization in the United States*. But in this year he was also fortunately able to make his final contribution to the study of literature proper, in discussions, firstly on Shelley, and secondly on Milton. With Milton he dealt in a short address at the unveiling of a window in St. Margaret's Church at Westminster. He could not, in the time available, discuss Milton's powerful handling of the difficult matter of a Puritan epic in *Paradise Lost*. And the Milton of religious and political controversy was often disfigured by want of amenity, by acerbity. But that of all our English race Milton is by his diction and rhythm the one artist of the highest rank in the great style whom we have; this he takes for certain. The mighty power of poetry and art resides chiefly in the refining and elevation wrought in us by the high and rare excellence of the great style. No race needs the influences of refining and elevation more than ours; and in poetry and art our grand source for these is Milton. The article on Shelley was a long one. Unfortunately Arnold was too much upset by the anarchic and often squalid details of Shelley's personal life, as revealed in the *Life* by Edward Dowden which he was reviewing, to deal adequately with his poetry. 'What a set! what a world!' Only at the end does he turn to 'our ideal Shelley, the angelic Shelley', who still may delight us, to the 'perfect gentleman, entirely without arrogance or aggressive egotism', of 'reverent enthusiasm for the great and wise, of high and tender seriousness, of heroic generosity, and of a delicacy in rendering services which was equal to his generosity'. Arnold's last word, indeed, is on the charm of Shelley's poetry. It is this which for many people establishes him as an angel.

Of his poetry I have not space now to speak. But let no one suppose that a want of humour and a self-delusion such as Shelley's have no effect upon a man's poetry. The man Shelley, in very truth, is not entirely sane, and Shelley's poetry is not entirely sane either. The Shelley of actual life is a vision of beauty and radiance, indeed, but availing nothing, effecting nothing. And in poetry, no less than in life, he is 'a beautiful *and ineffectual* angel, beating in the void his luminous wings in vain'.

The last year of Arnold's life had now come. He had long been in poor health, and since 1885 he had suffered from heart trouble. Probably his travels to America in 1883 and 1886 and the strain of lecturing had contributed to it, but both his father and his grandfather had died from a similar cause. On 15 April 1888 he was expecting to meet his daughter Lucy, who was due to arrive at Liverpool for a visit. He was hurrying to meet her, when, according to Mrs. Sellar, he leapt over a low fence, and dropped down dead. And as an undergraduate he could leap over the Wadham railings. He was buried at Laleham with his three boys. Before his death he had collected much of his recent writing in a second series of his *Essays in Criticism*. It was published posthumously with a short prefatory note by his old friend, Lord Coleridge. '*Inane munus* indeed, but all that a friend can do.'

VIII

ARNOLD'S PERSONALITY

Eᴀʀʟɪᴇʀ chapters have recorded the vagaries of Arnold's boyhood, his light-hearted days as undergraduate, his enduring affection for Oxford and the country around it, his long friendship with Clough, and the 'airs' and reticences which accompanied his slow progress to a considered outlook on life. His work as a School Inspector, and his literary writings in poetry and prose have also been sufficiently discussed. But something must now be said in conclusion of his matured personality, his affections, his character, his habits, his tastes and interests, his likes and dislikes. Much material is available in the two volumes of his *Letters*, published by George W. E. Russell, after his death, in 1895. They can, to some extent, be supplemented from other sources.

Mrs. Humphry Ward describes his personal appearance in his later years, 'the face, strong and rugged, the large mouth, the broad lined brow, and vigorous coal-black hair'. He was not like either of his parents. She thinks he may have inherited a Celtic strain from the Delafields. Perhaps the most notable thing in his character was his strong sense of family feeling. Russell said in his *Matthew Arnold* of 1904 that the excision from his *Letters* of what was thought too personal for publication had led to the result that he appeared not to have cared so much for his wife as for his own family and children. This, he said, must seem absurd 'to anyone who knew the beauty of that long honeymoon'. I do not think, however, that the *Letters* really give any such false impression. In 1866, for example, Arnold wrote, 'This is our wedding day. We have been fifteen years married, and it seems as if it was only last week', and in 1871 again, 'It seems only a year or two ago we were married'.

He rejoices that all his family took so to his wife, and she
to them. They had six children. The eldest was Thomas
born in 1852, and named after his grandfather. Then
came in 1853 Trevenen William, generally called Budge
and in 1855 Richard Penrose, similarly called Diddy and
later Dick. Then, after an interval, came the first girl,
Lucy Charlotte, in 1859. She was followed by Eleanor
Mary Caroline, in 1861. 'The new baby, or gorilla, as I
call her, is a fiend at night', wrote Arnold. The last of
all, after another long interval, was Basil Francis in 1866
Arnold played with them, and delighted in their humours
'Children', he wrote in 1861, 'are a great pleasure, or at
least I find mine so.' But with joys came griefs. Three of
the boys died in the lifetime of their parents. Basil died
in 1868. Thomas, always delicate, after a fall from his
pony in the same year, Trevenen in 1872. 'I enclose you
dear Matt's letter', wrote J. D. Coleridge to his father
'It is a most bitter and heavy blow. Forster told me he
was terribly cut up by it, but that his behaviour was
admirable. He had to be at an examination of pupil-
teachers, and Mr. Forster found him there with his poor
eyes full of tears, yet keeping order and doing his duty til
he could be relieved.' The three boys were all buried at
Laleham, as Arnold's father had been, and as he himself
was to be. The only remaining son, Richard, went from
Harrow to Balliol in 1874. Rather to his father's regret
he took History instead of Classics. Like his father he
seems to have been 'a bit of a lad'. In 1884 Matthew
hoped to make about £1,000 out of his American lectures
which would pay the main loan he had raised for his
son's Oxford debts. In 1882 Richard was living in
Liverpool. In 1904 he helped E. H. Coleridge in writing
his *Life* of Lord Coleridge. He visited Australia, married
there, on his return became a factory inspector, and died
in 1908. Lucy Arnold, later Whitridge, was dead by 1940
A son, Professor Arnold Whitridge, published some letter
of Arnold's in 1923, and a book on *Thomas Arnold of Rugby*

in 1928. Of two daughters, one was Eleanor, called in her babyhood Midget, the other Joan. Matthew's other daughter, also an Eleanor, became Mrs. Armine Wode-house by a first marriage, and Lady Sandhurst by a second. She compiled a *Matthew Arnold Birthday Book*, with a portrait, in 1883, and edited a selection from her father's *Notebooks* in 1902.

Many of the letters in Russell's collection were to Arnold's mother, who was living at Fox How. On her birthday in 1852 he wrote,

Accept every loving and grateful wish from a son to whom you have for nearly thirty years been such a mother as few sons have. The more I see of the world the more I feel thankful for the bringing up we had, so unworldly, so sound, and so pure.

I have already noted a letter in which he recognized her sympathetic comprehension of his writings on religion. He returned to this on her death in 1873. He regrets that he could not then find a wonderful letter which she wrote him on the publication of his *Literature and Dogma*.

I can think of no woman in the prime of life, brought up and surrounded as my mother was, and with my mother's sincere personal convictions, who could have written it; and in a woman past eighty it was something astonishing.

He quotes a letter to himself from Dean Stanley, on her reaction to her husband's death in 1842.

What to me was so impressive was not merely that she rose instead of sinking under the blow which we all feared would crush her, but that she retained the life-long reverence for your father's greatness, without a blind attempt to rest in the form and letter of his words.

A year after her death Arnold wrote to a sister of 'that central personage of our past—dearest mamma'.

We retain so much of her, she is so often in our thoughts, that she does not really pass away from us. She constantly comes into my mind.

It is, I think, characteristic of Arnold that his letters to his mother often contain kindly messages to one Rowland, her servant maid, who had been his nurse in his childhood.

Among the Arnolds of his own generation, Matthew's closest relations appear to have been with his brother Thomas, and his sister Jane, the 'K' of his letters and the 'Fausta' of his early poems. He admired her husband, W. E. Forster, the statesman. '*Integer*' was his word for him. There is an interesting letter to Jane in 1851.

How strong the tendency is, as characters take their bent, and lives their separate course, to submit oneself gradually to the silent influence that attaches us more and more to those whose characters are like ours, and whose lives are running the same way with our own, and that detaches us from everything besides. I am by nature so very different from you, the worldly element enters so much more largely into my composition, that as I become *formed* there seems to grow a gulf between us, which tends to widen till we can hardly hold any intercourse across it. But as Thomas à Kempis recommended, *frequenter tibi ipsi violentiam fac*, and as some philosopher advised to consort with our enemies because by them we were most surely apprised of our faults, so I intend not to give myself the rein in following my natural tendency, but to make war against it till it ceases to isolate me from you, and leaves me with the power to discern and adopt the good which you have and I have not.

But of all his brothers and sisters he writes with affection as 'dear old' Susy or Walter, or whichever it might be. The death of his brother William in 1859 was a grief to him. He always kept in touch with his grandmother's family, the Delafields.

His reverence for the memory of his father, always 'papa' in his letters to his mother, was great. He liked to write to her on the anniversaries of his birth and death. In some sense he seems to have thought that his own treatment of religious subjects was only a continuation of that which had ended in 1842. His father, he said, was the last free speaker of the Church of England clergy who spoke without being shackled, and without being ob- viously aware that he was so, and was in a false position in consequence. He worked in the direction of getting rid of all that was purely Semitic in Christianity, and was perhaps the only powerful Englishman of his day who did so. In fact he was the only deeply religious man who had the necessary culture for it. He notes his father's charming freedom of nature and humour. He thought that he had inherited from him a talent for pamphleteer- ing, and a deep sense of what, in the Greek and Roman world, was sound and rational. He came on an old letter containing careful plans for his own bringing up and that of his brothers and sisters.

We, who treat the matter so carelessly and lazily—we can hardly expect ours to do more than *grow up* at hazard, not be *brought up* at all. But this is just what makes him great—that he was not only a good man saving his own soul by righteous- ness, but that he carried so many others with him in his hand, and saved them, if they would let him, along with himself.

Arnold clung, too, to old friendships. One was Arthur Stanley, who had been a boy at Rugby, and in whose house later anything written by Matthew was 'kept as a treat for the evening'. He was a pall-bearer at Stanley's funeral in 1881. Another was with the Coleridges of Ottery St. Mary, of whom John Taylor had been his father's contemporary at Corpus, and John Dyke, after- wards Lord Coleridge, his own at Balliol. John Dyke, for all the *inane munus* of his *Prefatory Note* to the second series of Arnold's *Essays*, could be critical of him. They had a tilt in 1854. After Arnold's death Coleridge wrote,

It cannot be denied that he had the art, when he chose to use it, of making those whom he criticized look supremely ridicu- lous, and people put into such a position do not always see the fun of it so clearly as others. Nay, they are apt sometimes to get very angry, and to curse and swear (in a literary sense) so as to lay themselves open to fresh castigation from their amused

tormentor. All the more if the punishment is bestowed with
imperturbable good humour, with serene superiority, and with
an air of innocence and wonder, very funny but very exasperat-
ing. Doubtless he was habitually urbane, but there must be
many living men (and still more some dead ones) towards whom
contempt and indignation, rarely roused in him, are expressed
in language moderate indeed, but plain and direct to the very
verge of good manners.

Arnold could certainly be scathing in controversy. He
knew it himself. When engaged on his Celtic lectures in
1866 he wrote that he was glad to deal in sheer disquisition sometimes, and to 'leave irony and the Philistines'.
You have to hit hard in dealing with Philistines. In
private life he was both courteous and genial.

In 1863, on his birthday, he attempted an estimate of
his own character.

To-day I am forty-one, the middle of life in any case, and for
me, perhaps, much more than the middle. I have ripened, and
am ripening so slowly that I should be glad of as much time as
possible, yet I can feel, I rejoice to say, an inward spring which
seems more and more to gain strength, and to promise to resist
outward shocks, if they must come, however rough. But of this
inward spring one must not talk, for it does not like being talked
about, and threatens to depart if one will not leave it in mystery.

And in 1866, again on a birthday, he adds,

Forty-four is indeed an age at which one may say 'The time
past of our life may suffice us' to have trifled and idled, or
worse, in. I more and more become conscious of having something to do, and of a resolution to do it; and if I double my
present age, I shall, I hope, do something of it, but whether one
lives long or not, to be less and less *personal* in one's desires and
workings is the great matter, and this too I feel, I am glad to
say, more deeply than I did, but for progress in the direction of
the 'seeketh not her own' there is always room, up to the very
end, or, at least, near it.

Arnold's life in London from 1851 to 1866 was an
arduous one, and even when he had moved to West

Humble and then to Harrow, he had still often to be in town for a night. The constant travelling which his official duties as a School Inspector entailed was trying. From 1857 to 1867 he had also his lectures to prepare and deliver. In 1864, writing from the Athenaeum, he describes his daily occupations.

I work here at my *French Eton* from about eleven to three; then I write my letters; then I walk home and look over grammar papers till dinner; then dinner and a game of cards with the boys; then grammar papers for an hour and a half more; then an hour or half an hour's reading before bed.

In 1866 he had just finished a lecture, was not satisfied with it, and felt bilious and good for nothing. His health was always poor. Later in the year he was worried by an official report. He was getting on with it as badly as possible, in the hope that, when done, it would not be so bad. But little he did ever ran smooth or gave him satisfaction while he was about it. Later still he complained that his work spread and spread before him, and when he would be fairly through it he did not know. In January 1867 he records another daily programme.

At present I write a letter or two before breakfast, breakfast soon after nine, get here about half-past ten, write till half-past one, home for lunch, and go to skate for an hour; back here between three and four, work till seven, home to dinner, get to work again about half-past nine, and so on till twelve. Into this I manage to squeeze a little reading every day, but only a very little.

In April he was getting up soon after six every morning. His work was essential, since he was never a rich man. As late as 1870 he describes an interview with the Income Tax Commissioners, who had assessed his profits at £1,000 a year, on the ground that he was a distinguished literary man, and that his works must have a wide circulation. 'You see before you', he said, 'what you have often heard of, *an unpopular author*', and got the assessment reduced to £200. The London strain was aggravated by dinner parties. Both Arnold and his wife were sociable and hospitable by disposition, and liked to see their friends. Arnold, moreover, was something of an epicure, and particularly fond of venison. Sometimes, however, he made a resolution to avoid dinner parties, but found that he had to lay it aside. One thing he could not stand was having to make a speech after a public dinner. He had some amusements. He was a theatre-goer. He could play billiards. He skated. At one time he played croquet, but later gave it up. In 1885 lawn tennis proved too much for him. Going fast or uphill gave him the sense of having a mountain on his chest. He was not a smoker. That was the least humane thing about him. When he was in London the Athenaeum, to which he was elected, was a great resource. He looked forward with rapture to the use of its library, and found it a place at which he enjoyed 'something resembling beatitude'. He could do his work in a room consecrated to silence, and in another could discourse to his heart's content with his friends and even with some who were not his friends.

Arnold had a wide range of sympathies, and I think his likes were more numerous than his dislikes. But among the latter must certainly be included Gladstone. In early days Arnold had some admiration for him, as a politician, and Gladstone sent him a warm note on his *England and the Italian Question*. Later their politics diverged, especially on the Home Rule for Ireland problem. It was Gladstone, I think, of whom Arnold wrote in 1867,

> Respect is the very last feeling he excites in me; he has too little solidity and composure of character or mind for that. He is brilliantly clever, of course, and he is honest enough, but he is passionate and in no way great, as I think.

Russell, in his text of the letter, leaves the name of its subject a blank. In 1871 Arnold noted Gladstone's 'emotional verbiage' in Parliament. In 1876 he sent his

sister a note about Gladstone's admiration for one of his
articles, and added, 'It may burn'. During the same year
they met in the street. Gladstone asked him to tea. He
could not go. 'But his asking me shows his friendly feeling. I think at one time he positively disliked me.' Of
course they differed on religious questions. They met
again at dinner in 1877, and talked of Ireland, and again
somewhere in 1881, when the subject was Disraeli's
Endymion. With Disraeli himself Arnold also had inter-
mittent relations. They had met in early years, but did
not do so again until 1864, when they were staying in the
same house. Disraeli sat opposite Arnold at dinner,
'looking moody, black and silent', but Arnold thought
his face very striking. After dinner they talked together,
both of literature and of politics. Arnold recalled their
earlier meeting. Disraeli said he remembered it, and
added,

At that time I had a great respect for the name you bore, but
you yourself were little known. Now you are well known. You
have made a reputation, but you will go further yet. You have
a great future before you, and you deserve it.

Arnold bowed profoundly. I have noted Disraeli's jest
on 'sweetness and light' during a visit to Lord Chesham
at Latimer. There was another meeting there in 1872,
when Disraeli was very amiable. 'That famous Jew,
Dizzy', Arnold calls him. In 1877 he regrets that 'a
charlatan' like Dizzy should be Prime Minister. Later
in the year he saw Dizzy, 'elaborately got up', at the
Athenaeum, and in 1881 he had a long talk with him,
then Lord Beaconsfield, at a London dinner-party.
Arnold said he had told Gladstone of some epigrammatic
things in *Endymion*. Disraeli said, 'But I don't want to
talk about my things, I want to talk about *you*.'

He went on to say that he read me with delight, that I was
doing very great good, and ended by declaring that I was the
only living Englishman who had become a classic in his own

lifetime. The fact is that what I have done in establishing a number of current phrases—such as Philistinism, sweetness and light, and all that—is just the sort of thing to strike him.

Lord Salisbury Arnold thought a dangerous man, through his want of any true sense of literature and its beneficent functions. He knew religion and physical science, but nothing of the immense work between the two, which it was for literature to accomplish. John Morley, who had criticized him, he thought had learnt something from him, and knew it. Cardinal Newman he met at the Duke of Norfolk's house in 1880. He went because he wanted to have spoken to him once in his life. He made a deferential bow, and Newman took his hand and was charming. He said, 'I ventured to tell the Duchess I should like to see you.' One of his dislikes was Carlyle, whose writings, however, had influenced him in his early days. Others were Thackeray, whom, incidentally, he did not think a great writer, and Harriet Martineau—'what an unpleasant life and unpleasant nature!' Ruskin he thought in 1856 'febrile, irritable, and weak', and in 1863 said he should never like him. His sister Jane said he was becoming as dogmatic as Ruskin. He answered that the difference was that Ruskin was 'dogmatic and wrong'. But in 1877 he admitted, 'I am getting to like him'. The roll of his personal friendships is too long for enumeration. They were enduring. To Wyndham Slade and Theodore Walrond, the comrades of his youth, he always clung. They were sometimes companions of his travels. A touching example of his faithfulness is in a letter on the death of Rotha Quillinan, Wordsworth's grand-daughter.

It was impossible to know her without being fond of her, and I had known her almost all my life. I always continued to think of her as of one young, loving-hearted and simple, as she appeared to me when I first saw her at Rydal, forty years ago.

Arnold's physical appearance can best be judged from the portrait by G. F. Watts in the National Portrait

Gallery. In 1872 he had a visit from Henry Coleridge, a son of John Taylor Coleridge.

I thought he would never have let my hand go; at last he said,—'Matt!!—I expected to see a white-headed old man'. I said that my white hairs were all internal.

So much for Arnold in his town days. But by instinct he was a countryman. At Harrow he had a garden of over an acre. He compares it favourably with the patches of raw garden round the modern villas. He worked in it himself, pruning his roses. The kitchen garden was the best part of it, with a great deal of wall, on which were trained fruit-trees. The Cobham garden was better still. Its cottage was a century old and surrounded with great old trees. Blackbirds and thrushes sang indefatigably in it. Nightingales had deserted it, but swarmed in the lanes all round. In 1887 he said he had sometimes talked of ending his days in Florence, but found he could not uproot himself from his cottage and garden. He kept pets, which were his own as well as his children's. Atossa, generally called Toss, and Blacky were cats. Rover, Max, Geist, and Kaiser were dogs. Geist was a dachshound. Kaiser should have been, but proved to be a mongrel, partly a collie. Matthias was a canary. When they died, he wrote elegies on them.

During his mother's lifetime he generally managed to spend part of his holidays at Fox How. His son Richard called it 'the House of Paradise'. Later he was less often there. The district had become full of tourists, although they kept to the roads and lakes, and you could still wander over Loughrigg without meeting a soul. In 1864 he was taking holidays in Wales and the Scottish Highlands. But he had inherited his father's love for foreign travel. His official visits for the Education Office in 1859 and 1860, 1865, and 1885–6 were not enough to satisfy this. There were many shorter trips, to Belgium, to Switzerland, to the lakes of northern Italy. Sometimes he went alone, but did not like it. Generally his wife was with him, and in later years one or more of his children. His old Oxford friends, Theodore Walrond and Wyndham Slade, were also sometimes companions. When at home, he had many invitations to country houses. In 1863 he said that he disliked the life in them, with its endless talking and radical want of occupation. Nevertheless he accepted the invitations, and apparently enjoyed the visits, especially in his later years. He did not hunt, and was a bad shot. But there was often fishing, which had been the favourite sport of his youth. He often enumerates his catches, and sometimes there were fellow guests of importance to be talked to. It is worth noting that one of the houses to which he was most frequently asked was that of the rich Jew, Sir Anthony Rothschild, at Aston Clinton (Bucks.). He went also to that of the Meyer Rothschilds at Mentmore (Bucks.). Other hosts were Lord Derby, as far away as Knowsley (Lancs.), Lord Rosebery at Durdans (Surrey), which he found the warmest home in England, M. E. Grant Duff, once the Governor of Madras, at Hampden (Bucks.), Lord Chesham at Latimer (Bucks.), Lord Cowper at Panshanger (Herts.), the Duke of Bedford at Chenies (Bucks.), Lord Lytton at Knebworth (Herts.), Lord Lovelace at East Horsley (Surrey), Lord Pembroke at Wilton (Wilts.), Sir Trevor Lawrence at Dorking (Surrey), and W. J. Evelyn at Wotton (Surrey). Arnold was especially interested by an *Herbarium* collected by John Evelyn, during the seventeenth century, in Italy. He was himself an ardent botanist, and wherever he went, at home or abroad, made careful notes of the trees, shrubs, and flowers he came across. Almost his last letter says, 'Think of me when the tulip-tree comes into blossom in June'. But by June he was gone.

THE ARNOLD PEDIGREE

I. THE DELAFIELD FAMILY

—Delafield

Martha = William Arnold   Frances   Brother (unnamed)
ob. 1829   *ob.* 1801   *ob.* 1836   *ob.* 1820

II. SONS OF WILLIAM ARNOLD

William (*supra*)

Matthew *ob.* 1820   Thomas = (1820) Mary, d. John Penrose and Jane Trevenen
                      n. 1795
                      ob. 1842
William *ob.* 1806

n. 1791
ob. 1873

III. DAUGHTERS OF WILLIAM ARNOLD

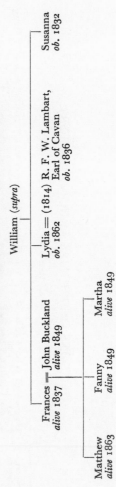

William (*supra*)

Frances = John Buckland   Lydia = (1814) R. F. W. Lambart,   Susanna
alive 1837   *alive* 1849   *ob.* 1862   Earl of Cavan   *ob.* 1832
                                               ob. 1836

Fanny *alive* 1849   Martha *alive* 1849

Matthew *alive* 1863

IV. SONS OF THOMAS ARNOLD (SENIOR)

Thomas (*supra*)

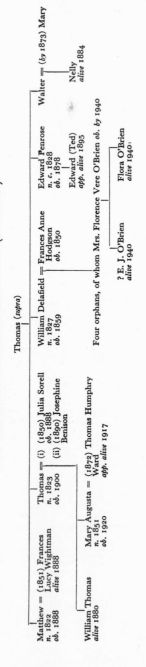

Matthew = (1851) Frances
n. 1822   Lucy Wightman
ob. 1888 *alive* 1888

Thomas = (i) (1850) Julia Sorell
n. 1823   *ob.* 1888
ob. 1900 (ii) (1890) Josephine
                 Benison

William Delafield = Frances Anne
n. 1827   Hodgson
ob. 1859   *ob.* 1850

Edward Penrose
n. c. 1828
ob. 1878

Walter = (by 1873) Mary
                    alive 1884

Nelly
alive 1884

William Thomas
alive 1880

Mary Augusta = (1872) Thomas Humphry
n. 1851   Ward
ob. 1920   *app. alive* 1917

Edward (Ted)
app. alive 1895

Four orphans, of whom Mrs. Florence Vere O'Brien *ob. by* 1940

?E. J. O'Brien
alive 1940

Flora O'Brien
alive 1940'

V. DAUGHTERS OF THOMAS ARNOLD (SENIOR)

Thomas (*supra*)

Jane Martha = (1850) William Edward
n. 1821   Forster
ob. 1899   n. 1818
                          ob. 1886

Mary = (i) (c. 1847) William Aldred
n. c. 1827   Twining *ob.* 1848
           (ii) (1858) J. S. Hiley

Frances Bunsen
Trevenen Whateley
n. 1833
alive 1916

Susanna = (c. 1853) John W.
n. 1835   Cropper
alive 1884

Francie
alive 1871

VI. SONS OF MATTHEW ARNOLD

Matthew (*supra*)

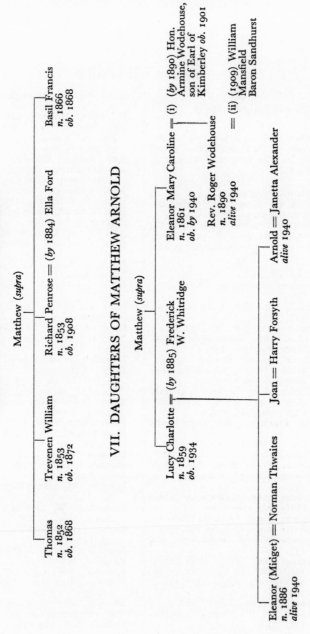

Thomas
n. 1852
ob. 1868

Trevenen William
n. 1853
ob. 1872

Richard Penrose = (*by* 1884) Ella Ford
n. 1853
ob. 1908

Basil Francis
n. 1866
ob. 1868

VII. DAUGHTERS OF MATTHEW ARNOLD

Matthew (*supra*)

Lucy Charlotte = (*by* 1885) Frederick W. Whitridge
n. 1859
ob. 1934

Eleanor Mary Caroline = (i) (*by* 1890) Hon. Armine Wodehouse, son of Earl of Kimberley *ob.* 1901
n. 1861
ob. by 1940
= (ii) (1909) William Mansfield Baron Sandhurst

Rev. Roger Wodehouse
n. 1890
alive 1940

Eleanor (Midget) = Norman Thwaites
n. 1886
alive 1940

Joan = Harry Forsyth

Arnold = Janetta Alexander
alive 1940

CLASSIFIED INDEX

I

THE ARNOLD FAMILY

II

MATTHEW'S VERSE

III

MATTHEW'S PROSE

IV
SELECTIONS

V
LETTERS

VI
THE EDUCATION OFFICE

VII

CONTEMPORARIES

VIII
EARLIER WRITERS

IX
LOCALITIES